USING cc:MAIL

**Featuring dozens of tips, tricks, and techniques
for getting the most from your cc:Mail system.
Covers both PC and Macintosh versions.**

Stephen M. Caswell

USING CC:MAIL

Featuring dozens of tips, tricks, and techniques for getting the most from your cc:Mail system. Covers both PC and Macintosh versions.

M&T BOOKS

 **M&T Books**
A Division of M&T Publishing, Inc.
501 Galveston Drive
Redwood City, CA 94063

© 1991 by M&T Publishing, Inc.

Printed in the United States of America

Limits of Liability and Disclaimer of Warranty
The Author and Publisher of this book have used their best efforts in preparing the book and the programs contained in it. These efforts include the development, research, and testing of the theories and programs to determine their effectiveness.

The Author and Publisher make no warranty of any kind, expressed or implied, with regard to these programs or the documentation contained in this book. The Author and Publisher shall not be liable in any event for incidental or consequential damages in connection with, or arising out of, the furnishing, performance, or use of these programs.

Library of Congress Cataloging in Publication Data

Caswell, Stephen A.
    Using cc:Mail / by Stephen A. Caswell
      p.   cm.
    Includes index.
    ISBN 1-55851-184-9 : $24.95
    1.Electronic mail systems.   I.Title.
HE6239.E54C38 1991   91-3410
384.3'4--dc20   CIP

Trademarks:
All products, names, and services are trademarks or registered trademarks of their respective companies.

Cover Design: Lauren Smith Design   **Editor:** Barry Parr

94 93 92 91   4 3 2 1

Contents

Why This Book Is For You

If you work in a corporate environment these days, you doubtless do at least some of your work on a computer. And if your computer is linked in any way to other computers in your building or company, it's likely you communicate with your co-workers via an electronic mail system. This book is about one such system, cc:Mail—a powerful program that lets you create text, graphics, and formatted messages, and send them not only to others on your mail system, but to users of other e-mail systems, and to fax machines.

Like most computer-based networks, your cc:Mail system is probably maintained in-house by a network administrator, referred to throughout this book as your cc:Mail administrator. Of course, between the on-call administrator and the user guide that comes with cc:Mail, you've probably been pretty successful at finding your way through the ins and outs of this multi-faceted system. This book is a hands-on tutorial for those who want to go beyond the manual and who don't want to have to schedule an appointment with an administrator every time they have a question or run into a glitch in their cc:Mail system. It includes an overview of the field of electronic mail, so that you will not only learn the specifics of how to use cc:Mail, but will understand where cc:Mail fits into the overall world of e-mail. You'll find:

- An overview of electronic mail, including the structure of e-mail systems and the relationship between computer mailbox systems, facsimile, and other e-mail technologies.

- A hands-on tutorial guide to cc:Mail that explores all of its commands and features for IBM PCs and compatibles and Macintosh computers.

- Detailed graphics that take you step-by-step through every feature of cc:Mail.

- A discussion of how a cc:Mail system can be interconnected with other cc:Mail systems, and with non-cc:Mail systems, to form an e-mail network.

- An exploration of potential e-mail applications.

Introduction

This book is about cc:Mail and the overall world of electronic mail in which cc:Mail operates. It is not about personal computers, local area networks (LANs), remote computers, or remote communication networks—which are the underlying technological devices and systems that allow electronic mail systems to exist. Nevertheless, it is important to have a working knowledge of these systems in order to understand electronic mail. Therefore, this book explores the underlying technologies that support electronic mail whenever it is relevant.

Required Background

To understand this book properly, you need only a minimal knowledge about your personal computer—whether it's an IBM PC or compatible or a Macintosh. You must know how to turn the computer on and off, and understand the basic components—i.e., RAM memory, hard disk, floppy disk, keyboard, monitor, etc. If your computer is an IBM PC or compatible, you should understand the basics of the DOS operating system, such as the directory structure, including subdirectories, and how to issue DOS commands from within the directory structure. If you use a Macintosh, you must know how to use the mouse to manipulate through the Finder to initiate programs, and also be familiar with desktop accessories.

You do not, however, need to have an understanding of LANs, modems, communication networks, e-mail gateways, or any of the other technologies underlying the cc:Mail system. In fact, one of cc:Mail's major benefits is that it makes the underlying communication networks as transparent as possible.

Conventions

During the course of this book, numerous references will be made to keystrokes and/or mouse movements.

Key Names and Labels. The names of all keys appear as they do on the keyboard, such as t, T, %, F1 or +. Keyboard action keys also appear in bold type as they appear on most keyboards, such as **Enter**, **Backspace**, **Spacebar**, **Ctrl**, **Shift**, **Del**, **Alt**, **Option**, **Ins**, **Esc**, etc. Not every keyboard uses the identical conventions for these keys. Some keyboards may use the word **RETURN** or a symbol for the **ENTER** key and may use a symbol to designate the **Backspace** key.

The Control key for IBM PCs, which is used to designate commands, will be designated **Ctrl** (for example, **Ctrl-S**). On Macintoshes, a cloverleaf key, called the Command Key, is used for the same purpose.

Key Combinations and Sequences. On occasion, you will need to press a sequence of keys together. In this book, these sequences will be designated with a hyphen, such as **Ctrl-Alt-Del**. The hyphen means that you should press all the keys in the sequence at the same time. A sequence with no hyphens, such as **Esc F4**, indicates that you should press the **Esc** key first and then press the **F4** key.

If a sequence of keys has a hyphen missing from the final key in the sequence, it means that the final key should be pressed after the hyphenated keys. For example, **Alt-Spacebar C** means that you should press the **Alt** and **Spacebar** keys simultaneously, and then press the **C**.

Entering Commands. When you are expected to enter commands, the words to be typed will appear in all caps and in boldtype, such as **MAIL** or **INSTALL**. If you are expected to type a command and an example is shown, it will be in all caps after the appropriate DOS prompt. Do not type the DOS prompt symbol, which will be designated as A>, B> or C>.

For both Macintosh and IBM PC users, all mouse commands will be expressed as a command to click, such as click once or double-click. Unless otherwise noted, the mouse click instruction means to click the leftmost button. Mouse movement instructions will have the words move, drag or point associated with them, such as "move the mouse to the cc:Mail program icon and double-click the mouse button," "drag any unwanted messages to the trash can," or "point at a command."

The move command means move the mouse to a designated place on the screen.

The drag command means press the mouse button down on an object and keep it pressed down while moving the object by moving the mouse. The point command means move the mouse until the pointer symbol designates a specific command or screen location.

How This Book Is Organized

The book is organized into six sections: Introduction to cc:Mail, cc:Mail for PCs, cc:Mail Remote, cc:Mail for the Macintosh, cc:Mail for Windows, and the Appendices.

Section 1—Introduction to cc:Mail. This section has two chapters which explain how electronic mail systems are structured and designed. If you are new to electronic mail, you will find these chapters very useful because they explore the architecture underlying not only cc:Mail, but almost every e-mail product on the market.

Section 2—cc:Mail for PCs. This section explores using cc:Mail on IBM PCs or compatibles running DOS. The section is broken into seven chapters.

Chapters 3–9 review the main features of cc:Mail step-by-step. Chapter 3 is an overview of using cc:Mail, including how to install the cc:Mail program and begin operations. Chapter 4 explores reading and responding to messages. Chapter 5 shows you how to create and send messages. Chapter 6 explores retrieving messages that are stored in bulletin boards, folders, or personal archives. Chapter 7 shows you how to manage your cc:Mail mailbox, including creating mailing lists and folders, and changing your password. Chapter 8 explores cc:Mail's two TSR (Terminate and Stay Resident) programs: Notify and Messenger. Chapter 9 discusses error messages you may receive while operating cc:Mail on a PC.

Section 3—cc:Mail Remote. This section explores the cc:Mail Remote program, which allows people who are on PCs removed from a LAN to exchange messages with regular cc:Mail users. cc:Mail Remote opens up cc:Mail to any user with an IBM PC or compatible and a modem. While cc:Mail Remote has the same look and feel as its regular version operating on a LAN, there are some very distinct differences, which are discussed in this section.

Chapter 10 examines the differences between cc:Mail Remote and the regular cc:Mail program. Chapter 11 explores the error messages you may receive while using cc:Mail Remote.

Section 4—cc:Mail for The Macintosh. Chapters 12–16 explore using cc:Mail on Macintosh computers. While IBM PC and Macintosh users can exchange messages, the user interfaces are so distinct that users are almost in two different, albeit interconnected, worlds.

Chapter 12 explains how to install cc:Mail and begin operations. Chapter 13 explores the basics of using cc:Mail on a Macintosh, including a discussion of its architecture, and a detailed description of management tasks such as changing your password, creating folders, and creating mailing lists. Chapter 14 describes how to read and respond to messages. Chapter 15 leads you through creating and sending messages. Chapter 16 explains error messages you may receive while using cc:Mail on a Macintosh.

Section 5—cc:Mail for Windows and Beyond. cc:Mail, Inc. recently introduced a version of cc:Mail that operates in the Windows environment.

Chapter 17 examines cc:Mail's new Windows user interface. Chapter 18 explores where cc:Mail is headed as a product, particularly in light of cc:Mail's acquisition by Lotus Corp., and the recent strategic partnership between IBM and Lotus in which cc:Mail will play a significant role.

Section 6—Appendices. The appendices in this section are primarily associated with cc:Mail on PCs.

Appendix A talks about how to use the text editor when creating messages. Appendix B explores cc:Mail's graphics editor. Appendix C explains the unique cc:Mail Snapshot program that allows you to take screen snapshots within any application and have them attached to a cc:Mail message. Appendix D is a listing of every cc:Mail command on a menu-by-menu basis. Finally, Appendix E explores the cc:Fax program for sending and receiving faxes directly from cc:Mail.

Introduction to cc:Mail

USING CC: MAIL

CHAPTER 1

An Overview of Electronic Mail

If your goal in reading this book is solely to learn the specifics of using cc:Mail, you can skip to Chapter 2. If, however, you are new to the world of e-mail and/or you want to know more about e-mail in general and where cc:Mail fits in this world, this chapter is important.

Introduction

Electronic mail is a software system that uses one or more computers to transfer messages among users. These messages can be text files, graphics, sound, or executable programs.

E-mail, facsimile systems, and several other related technologies are all different species within the genus of electronic messaging systems that have existed since 1844, when Samuel F. B. Morse sent the first telegraph message, "What hath God wrought?" over an operating commercial system. While there certainly is overlap among some of the technologies, there are also sufficient differences to give each technology value in the market.

The following technologies are members of the genus of Electronic Messaging:

1. Telegraph

2. Telex/twx/teletex

3. Facsimile

4. E-mail

5. Voice mail

6. Computer conferencing

The Four T's of Electronic Messaging

The telegraph, telex, twx, and teletex are outdated technologies that are declining in usage. Telegraphy, of course, is the grandfather of electronic messaging, dating back to the 1800s.

Telex and its closely related cousin, twx, are also dying technologies—having been outflanked by the facsimile in the last few years. Telex messages are stored and forwarded in an electronic format, but the final message is text on paper. Telex sends characters at a rate of 6 per second to fixed terminals, while twx, which operates identically to telex, sends characters at a rate of 10 per second. Telex originated in the 1930s and was the first electronic messaging technology to be used by thousands of businesses worldwide. At its peak, around 1980, there were an estimated two million telex and twx terminals in the world. Today, the number of actual telex terminals has declined precipitously in industrialized countries to perhaps one million worldwide.

The final technology, teletex, was supposed to be the replacement for telex. Teletex was designed by a number of the telecommunication authorities worldwide; its significance ended when facsimile and e-mail burst onto the scene.

Facsimile

When the high-tech edition of "Trivial Pursuit" comes out, one of the showstoppers will be, "When was the fax first developed?" Believe it or not, facsimile was developed and patented in 1842 by a Scottish clock maker named Alexander Bain. While Bain may have invented the fax machine, the technology, at the time, lacked three key elements:

- An easy means of scanning the information.

- An effective method of printing.

- A low-cost communications network.

When Bain patented facsimile, an electronic communications network did not exist. As a result, facsimile could be used only locally within a facility. Bain also had no effective way to scan an original document. Because systems that use light beams were not in existence, he used raised letters that came in contact with a swinging metal pendulum. Information was transferred when the pendulum touched the raised letter, which closed an electronic circuit and sent a charge to an equivalent pendulum at the receiving site. Printing (recreating the image) was also a problem. Bain's fax machine used a specially coated paper that changed color when it received an electronic charge. While the paper worked, it was both expensive and cumbersome.

Despite numerous efforts to develop facsimile machines during the 1800s and 1900s, it took about 140 years for all of the elements of easy scanning, effective printing, and low-cost communications to fall into place. Until then, fax was a specialized technology used primarily to send press photos, fingerprints, and weather maps. Facsimile transmission of general-purpose business documents has been increasing steadily since the late 1960s.

The catalyst for facsimile was the development of today's modern fax machine, which offers a solid-state scanning system, thermal paper printing, and digital transmission of a typical page in 15 to 40 seconds for a price of about $500 to $1,000 per machine. The result has been staggering. Sales of fax machines have jumped from about 50,000 systems in 1982 to an anticipated 2.5 million machines in 1991.

The explosion in facsimile is creating an enormous base of what should be viewed as remote, electronic printing machines that reside in almost every business in North America. Today, these machines are typically accessed only by equivalent machines. They work by placing a document in the hopper, dialing a number, and then pressing the start button—much like a copier.

Increasingly, however, this base of remote printing machines will be accessed by computer systems with electronic cards that enable them to communicate as if they were fax machines. In this environment, fax machines will function as remote printers to the computer, spewing out documents as if they were connected locally to the computer.

Electronic Mail

Electronic mail, or e-mail, is the use of a computer to create a mailbox system in which messages are stored, to be accessed upon demand by the recipients. E-mail is also known as computer mailbox systems or computer-based message systems (CBMS). In fact, until the last year or two, e-mail was the designation for the entire field of electronic messaging. As an example, the Electronic Mail Association, whose headquarters are in Arlington, VA, once defined electronic mail as:

> The generic name for non-interactive communication of text, data, image, or voice messages between a sender and designated recipients by systems utilizing telecommunications links.

The definition was so broad that it intentionally included computer mailbox systems and facsimile as electronic mail systems. Increasingly, however, e-mail means the world of computer mailbox systems, which is considered a distinct world from facsimile. As you will see, the two technologies are blurring considerably. Nevertheless, in this book, e-mail is used to refer to computer mailbox systems, while facsimile is treated as a distinct technology.

E-mail systems were first developed in the late 1960s on mainframe computers, although the first commercial systems did not appear until the mid-1970s. In the 1970s and early 1980s, e-mail was dominated by systems that operated on mainframes and minicomputers. In the late 1980s, as Local Area Networks (LANs) began to proliferate, e-mail products designed to operate on LANs were introduced. cc:Mail, for example, was developed in late 1984 before the LAN movement had really begun. As LANs accelerated in the latter 1980s, LAN-based mail systems such as cc:Mail became far more popular.

Voice Mail

While most people consider voice mail to be very different from e-mail and facsimile, it is actually a closely related cousin to both. Like e-mail, voice mail stores messages in mailboxes and, in fact, operates identically to most e-mail systems; voice messages are stored instead of text or other computer-generated messages.

Like facsimile, however, the information is stored as a digitized stream; in fact, the same type of electronic chips and circuit cards are required to send fax and voice information.

Voice mail systems were first developed in the late 1970s, although the cost of disk storage made them very expensive. Basically, a voice mail system needs about 3,000 times the amount of storage to store the same amount of information as a text mail system.

Fortunately for voice mail, it evolved in a very different manner than either text mail or fax. Numerous businesses have added voice mail systems to their telephone switches, so that when a person is not available, a message is stored much as it is with a personal answering machine. As a result, while text mail is typically used for group communications within a business, and fax is used to send formal documents, voice mail is used to leave short, informal messages when a phone call does not connect, minimizing the cost of storing voice mail messages.

Computer Conferencing

The final type of electronic messaging—computer conferencing—is the most esoteric and, in many ways, the most powerful form of e-mail. Computer conferencing allows groups of individuals to use a computer to communicate together. In its simplest form, computer conferencing is organized as bulletin boards in which an individual can post a message to a board covering a specific topic, so that other individuals can read the aggregated comments and add their own comments.

In its most complex form, computer conferencing is organized so that people can hold extended meetings divided into numerous and related topics. Users can not only add their own comments, but formal votes can be taken via structured polls, with the results automatically tabulated by computer. In much the same way that e-mail or fax automates the sending of memos within a company, a good computer conferencing system can eliminate the need for people to meet face-to-face. Conferencing has become very popular on home information services, such as CompuServe and Prodigy, and on informal bulletin board systems.

Summary of Electronic Messaging Technologies

The above summary of electronic messaging technologies is just that—a brief summary. Its purpose is to point out that there are multiple technologies within the genus of electronic messaging. Today, these technologies typically operate in separate systems, such as an e-mail system, fax machine, or voice mail system. One of the key trends of the 1990s, however, will be for these technologies to be combined, so that fax is merged with e-mail in one system, or voice mail and fax are combined together. Those who may favor one technology over another should keep in mind that we are in the beginning stages of the electronic messaging revolution; what we're seeing today is primitive in comparison to what's coming.

To get an idea of the magnitude of the changes that will take place in the next ten years, think back to 1980. There were no IBM PCs and compatibles. All we had was the Apple II and 8-bit CP/M machines using 64 to 128 kilobytes of RAM. Today, we have 32-bit machines, 4-megabyte RAM chips, graphics interfaces, laser printers, and LANs. Given that the pace of technology is hastening, not slowing down, it's obvious that there will be more changes during the next ten years than there were from 1980 to 1990.

The Rise of Electronic Mail

E-mail was developed first on mainframes and minicomputers, primarily as a means of allowing the computer scientists who used these machines to communicate with each other. The earliest e-mail systems were based on very simple utilities that allowed messages to be created, transmitted, and read. As the researchers looked more closely at what they were creating, they started to take a more formal approach to the design of e-mail systems.

The Internal Memo/Post Office Model

Understanding e-mail is very simple. All you need is some familiarity with standard office memos and the postal service. All e-mail systems in operation today are based on these two related models.

Think of e-mail messages as office memos, and the delivery system as the post office. If you're a little afraid of using e-mail because it has something to do with computers, this should take the fear away.

All e-mail systems are based on the structure of a standard memo:

Command: **mail**

Welcome to the Corporate E-Mail System
March 14, 1984

You have one new message.

Command: **inbox**

No	From	Date	Subject	Length
1	J.Jones	3-14-84	Next Meeting	244 chs

Command: **read 1**

Date:	3-14-84
To:	S. Smith
	B.Parks

CC: C.Carlson

Subject: Next Meeting

The next meeting of the planning committee will be held on March 21. We need to know if you will be able to attend so we may schedule you in the agenda to make a presentation. Please reply by March 16. Thank you.

Jeff

Command: **reply**

Please enter text of reply. End with a period on a separate line.

I will be able to attend on the 21st. I'll be ready with my presentation on our plans for the next quarter.

Paul

.

Command: **Forward**

To: **R.Wilson**

CC:

Comments.

Randy, get ready for the meeting next week. We're on the agenda and I want you to make half the presentation on our next quarter's plans.

Paul

Command: **bye**

Mail session now over.

The Post Office Structure

When an office worker is at his or her desk, the postal system that supports the memo structure is invisible, but a complex structure moves memos between the desks of employees within a company and to other companies. The system typically operates on a floor-by-floor basis. A designated employee collects all memos on a particular floor, and separates memos for employees on that floor from memos for employees on other floors, or at other facilities. Memos for local employees are put in their mail slots for later delivery, while memos for remote employees are sent to the mailroom for further sorting and delivery.

The further away memos can be sent, the more complex the mailing structure. Typically, a company's mailroom has two separate mail streams—intra-company and inter-company. Intra-company mail is usually put into slots for delivery within each floor of the facility, or into private mailbags that are delivered by trucks that run between the firm's different facilities. Inter-company mail is sent to the postal service, which acts as a public memo delivery system so that memos sent between people in different companies are delivered properly.

Two important—almost unstated—parts of a company's mail-delivery structure are the addressing system and directory that many people must use so that mail can be delivered properly. Figure 1-1 shows the structure of a typical paper-based mail delivery system.

Structure of an E-Mail System

An e-mail system has an almost identical structure to the inbox/outbox postal structure described above, except that all of these features are created electronically inside the computer. This is where people get into trouble in understanding e-mail. However, all e-mail systems are basically the same—a memo-creation system and a delivery system in which messages to be sent are placed in an outbox, while messages to be received are put in an Inbox. Once messages are read, they can be left in the Inbox or placed in a separate file. While messages are being read, they can be replied to, forwarded, or tossed (deleted).

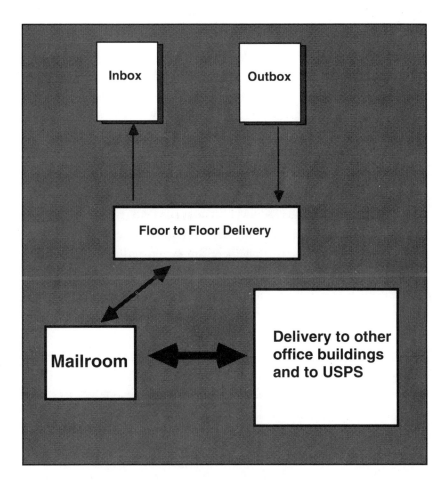

Figure 1-1. Structure of a typical paper-based mail delivery system

Mainframe/Minicomputer Mail Systems

In the early days of e-mail, a mainframe computer or minicomputer was programmed for the e-mail application. Users were often in other buildings. As a result, the e-mail applications were set up so that users could dial into the computer using a terminal or terminal-emulator program in a PC. Users interacted with the computer in what was called line-oriented mode. The user would be given a prompt by the computer and asked to give a command to perform the next action. Interaction with the computer was limited to single commands.

Popular Mainframe/Minicomputer E-Mail Systems

During the late 1980s, a number of popular mainframe and minicomputer mail systems emerged. Many systems, particularly the public services, had line-oriented interfaces, while others, particularly those used inside companies, had screen-oriented interfaces that were easier to use. In all cases, they worked on the model of a memo, inbox/outbox, and postal system.

For intra-company communications, the successful e-mail systems were based on the most popular mainframes and minicomputers. IBM had PROFS, Digital Equipment had VMSMail and All-in-One Mail, Data General had CEO, Hewlett-Packard had HPMail, and UNIX had UNIXMail. Today, EMMS (Electronic Mail & Micro Systems) newsletter, which is published by International Resource Development of New Canaan, CT, estimates that there are seven million e-mail users operating on in-house mainframe and minicomputer systems. E-mail always rides on the popular computers and communication networks that a company is installing, because it is too expensive to install a separate network of computers and communication lines just for e-mail.

For inter-company business communications, users have signed up with public e-mail services, such as MCI Mail from MCI, AT&T Mail from AT&T, SprintMail (formerly Telemail) from US Sprint, Dialcom from British Telecom, Quik-Comm from GE Information Services, and several other smaller public e-mail services. EMMS newsletter estimates that there are about 915,000 users on these services, while there are also about 1.4 million users on the home-oriented services offered by CompuServe, IBM/Sears, and GE. In the home-oriented services, mail is one of many services available, including bulletin boards, home shopping, database access, etc.

LAN Mail Systems

In the late 1980s, e-mail systems were developed for the growing world of LANs. These mail systems had several advantages over minicomputer and mainframe-based systems:

- The user interface was far superior.

- Users were notified almost immediately when messages were received, which was far more convenient than having to log in several times a day to check for mail.

- The company incurred only minimal hardware costs because a mainframe or minicomputer did not have to be dedicated to running e-mail. Instead, e-mail ran on multiple lower-cost PCs.

- Communication costs declined considerably because only messages destined for remote locations had to be sent remotely. Mainframe and minicomputers, on the other hand, had to be accessed from remote locations to send all messages.

While LAN mail systems have some clear advantages over mainframe and minicomputer-based e-mail systems, there are also some disadvantages:

- One LAN mail node, or post office, typically only supports a relatively small number of users. In order to create a network within a large organization, multiple LAN mail post offices must be linked together, requiring careful coordination.

- A single directory of users must be managed across multiple LAN mail post offices, so that communication is transparent.

- LAN mail is available only when a LAN is already installed. Few companies install a LAN specifically to offer e-mail. They install LANs for other reasons, such as to share peripherals and to access a common set of data, and then discover the value of e-mail.

In short, while LAN mail systems offer substantial advantages in terms of ease-of-use and convenience versus mainframe and minicomputer-based e-mail systems, LAN mail systems require very careful planning and coordination in order to be implemented successfully across a large organization. Once a LAN is installed, however, LAN mail is a very cost-effective alternative to using a corporate mainframe or minicomputer, particularly since most LAN mail systems today can be linked by a gateway to the corporate mail system and to public services, so that a user requires only one mailbox.

To testify to the growing popularity of LAN mail systems, EMMS newsletter estimates that there are more than four million e-mail users on LAN mail systems. Figure 1-2 shows the growth of all types of e-mail systems during the last five years.

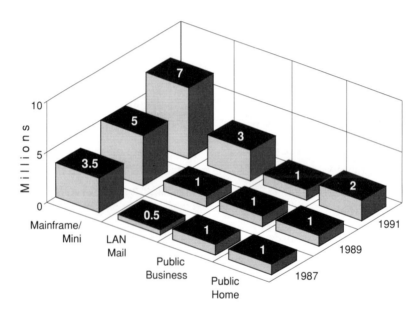

Source: EMMS Newsletter

Figure 1-2. Growth of different types of e-mail systems between 1987-1991

Growth of Electronic Mail

As the figure shows, while e-mail on mainframes and minicomputers has grown steadily, e-mail on LANs has virtually exploded and is now growing at more than 100 percent annually.

cc:Mail in the Market

The cc:Mail LAN mail system was one of the first on the market and today is the leading LAN mail system, with more than 1 million users. While the world of LAN mail may be growing very rapidly, cc:Mail is a mature, highly reliable product that has gone through several versions of development. cc:Mail has all of the key features critical to an e-mail system, along with a number of features that go beyond what is available in most e-mail systems.

cc:Mail is the leader in the market in allowing multifile messages and was the first to allow text and graphics to be merged in a standard message. While this may not sound particularly significant, it has very important implications for the evolution of cc:Mail as a product, particularly in the area of integration with facsimile. The following chapters explore the inner workings of cc:Mail in detail.

USING CC: MAIL

CHAPTER 2

An Overview of cc:Mail

cc:Mail is an electronic mail program that operates over local area networks (LANs). cc:Mail allows its users to send and receive mixed text/graphics messages and attached computer files. cc:Mail assigns each user an ID, and then stores and tracks the messages sent to and from each ID.

cc:Mail consists of two fundamental elements: a "post office" database that resides on the LAN server, and a "user agent" program that runs on each user's personal computer.

The post office database is the central storage repository that represents a physical post office. The post office contains all messages that are created and stored in either an Inbox or set of private folders designated by the user. Each registered user has an Inbox and up to 200 private folders. The post office database also stores messages destined for other cc:Mail post offices and/or other e-mail systems as required, although this is an optional capability.

User agent software allows users to create messages, including attached files, and allows them to log on to the post office to read their Inboxes and/or personal folders, and to send messages. While the post office resides on a server on the LAN, the user agent software operates on each person's computer.

Operating on a LAN

A LAN is a high-speed environment that connects nearby personal computers together. A typical LAN has from 5 to 50 personal computers attached to it, and operates at speeds that range from as low as 256,000 bits per second (bps) to as high as 100 Mbps. If you have a Macintosh, your LAN probably communicates at 256 Kbps. If you have an IBM PC, your LAN probably runs at 10 Mbps. Don't worry about the speed of the LAN. As long as it is engineered properly, it will be fast enough to handle your e-mail application.

The key point to understand about cc:Mail operating on a LAN is that "communication" takes place when users access a hard disk on the mail server (which is another computer) as if the disk were located at the user's computer (see **Figure 2-1**). cc:Mail stores all user messages at its post office server. When a user checks his Inbox, for example, the command is sent down the LAN to the post office server, which keeps a file on the server's hard disk with the Inbox information about that user. The information is sent back across the LAN to the user's personal computer and displayed on the user's screen.

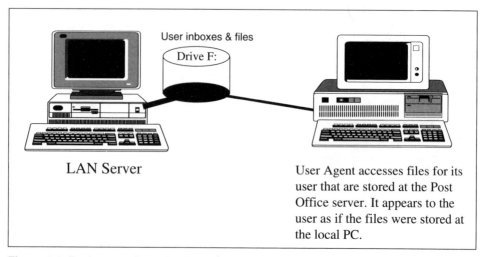

User inboxes & files

Drive F:

LAN Server

User Agent accesses files for its user that are stored at the Post Office server. It appears to the user as if the files were stored at the local PC.

Figure 2-1. Basic operation of LAN Mail

Reading and sending messages involve similar processes. A message is created in the user's personal computer. When the message is sent, the information travels down the LAN to the server, where it is stored until it is read by the recipient(s). Attached files (a copy, not the original) are also sent to the LAN server and are stored with their constituent messages.

cc:Mail Post Offices

A cc:Mail post office stores all of the electronic mail messages for its local users. In effect, a cc:Mail post office gives each local user a mailbox at a central post office location, and also stores all of his e-mail-related files. A cc:Mail post office has some special security features, making it difficult for an unauthorized user to log in to read someone else's mail, or walk up to the post office's server and use local computer commands to read mail. Each user creates a password to protect unauthorized access, and all cc:Mail messages are encrypted when they're stored on computer disk.

The post office program can run on an IBM PC or compatible running under DOS, Windows or OS/2, or on a Macintosh. Typically, the post office must operate on a LAN, although it is possible to operate a cc:Mail network of remote users who dial in to a stand-alone PC. cc:Mail works with virtually all popular LAN operating environments, such as Novell, LAN Manager, 3+OPEN for IBM PCs, and the AppleTalk LAN for Macintosh computers using an AppleShare-compatible file server. In LAN environments where PCs and Macintosh computers can coexist, cc:Mail works transparently across both computer families, so IBM PC and Macintosh users can exchange messages without even knowing which machines are used by which people. In fact, you can access your mailbox from either a PC or a Macintosh.

When a cc:Mail post office is equipped with gateway software, it also serves as the central clearinghouse for messages that must go beyond the local group of cc:Mail users. Gateway software allows the post office to connect to:

- Other cc:Mail post offices.

- Remote users who access a specific post office.

- Public e-mail services, such as MCI Mail.

- Other LAN-based e-mail programs that use the Message Handling System (MHS) protocol.

- Popular mainframe and minicomputer-based mail systems, such as IBM's PROFS and Digital's All-in-One.

- Soft-Switch Central, which is a program widely used in large companies for linking multiple e-mail systems together.

- Mail systems that use the X.400 international e-mail interconnection standard.

- Fax machines around the world.

In short, cc:Mail is more than a program that allows a small number of users on a LAN to send e-mail to each other. When the cc:Mail post office is configured with the appropriate gateway software, it allows cc:Mail users to exchange messages with an almost unlimited number of users, as shown in **Figure 2-2**.

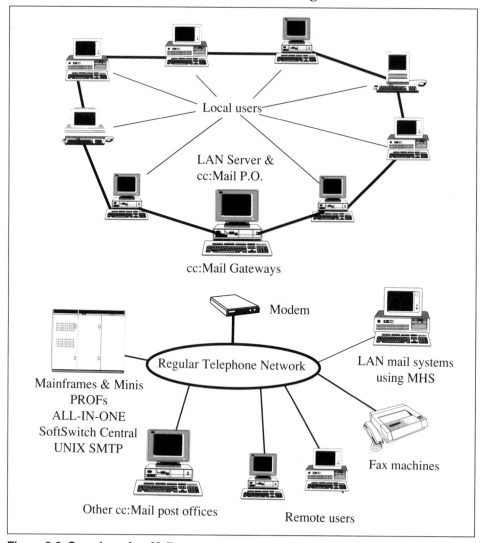

Figure 2-2. Overview of cc:Mail

Transparent Communications Across Gateways

An important part of cc:Mail is the ability for its users to communicate transparently to everyone, including those on other e-mail systems, as if all users were connected to the same local post office. The cc:Mail post office is configured with a directory that can house the names of local users, as well as users on remote systems.

cc:Mail automatically updates addresses for all post offices on the network, making it easy to maintain an entire directory of users throughout an organization. This includes lists of users on non-cc:Mail systems such as IBM's PROFS, MCI Mail, or any other mail system across a cc:Mail gateway. As long as these addresses are maintained in one cc:Mail post office, all changes will be disseminated to all cc:Mail post offices.

cc:Mail's directory feature makes communications completely transparent—a concept that is very important to the use of e-mail, especially on LAN-based systems. You send a message to a user by name, not address. When a cc:Mail user sends a message, he or she doesn't have to worry about whether it is a local or remote message. The cc:Mail post office handles it. The user sends local and remote messages in exactly the same way. Also, cc:Mail users are notified in exactly the same fashion whether a message was received locally or from a remote system.

When setting up a cc:Mail account, the user has the option of using a separate program to automatically check the server for new messages. cc:Mail notifies the user when a message is received, regardless of what program he or she is using locally. The notification takes place whether the message was sent from the person who sits in the next office, or from someone in another continent on a remote e-mail system.

When a cc:Mail user sends a message, he or she sees a directory listing of all users registered on the local server, whether they are local or remote. The directory also includes a listing of all remote mail systems on the network. The process of creating and sending messages is identical, whether the recipient is local or remote, which gives the sender the perception that all users are as close as the local cc:Mail post office.

Bulletin Boards and Mailing Lists

While cc:Mail and other LAN e-mail programs are noted for their individual-to-individual communications, cc:Mail also has a limited bulletin board capability that lets you send messages to public bulletin boards set up by a cc:Mail administrator. Bulletin boards are open to all users, both local and remote, assigned to a specific post office. cc:Mail's bulletin board capability is relatively limited compared to other BBS systems, particularly those that operate on public services, such as CompuServe, because cc:Mail's bulletin boards cannot be nested in the topic and subtopic relationship that is common to most BBSs.

cc:Mail's mailing list capability is another highly effective way to achieve group communications as well as individual-to-individual communications. A mailing list is a list of recipients for a single message. There are two types of mailing lists: public and private. Public lists are created by the cc:Mail administrator and are open to any user. An example of such a mailing list might be the names of members of a specific committee within your organization. Each user creates private lists by selecting addresses from the directory.

cc:Mail User Agent Programs

Messages are created, sent, and read by programs that operate on each user's personal computer. These programs, called user agents, are available for IBM PCs or compatibles and Macintoshes. Whether the user is communicating with a post office that operates on a Macintosh or on an IBM PC or compatible, a cc:Mail user agent includes:

- An Inbox that displays incoming messages.

- A text editor that allows text messages to be created. The IBM PC version of cc:Mail has a special graphics editor, so that text and graphics can be included in the same message, and also has a "snapshot" capability that allows the user to capture any screen display and mail it like any other cc:Mail message.

- An "enclose" feature, so that formatted and binary files can be attached to cc:Mail messages.

- A mailing list feature that allows each user to create a set of private mailing lists, while also accessing public lists created by the cc:Mail administrator.

- A set of folders that can be created by each user to store messages that have been received or created. Each user can have up to 200 private folders.

- A background utility program that checks the cc:Mail post office at a specified interval, such as every ten minutes, to determine if new mail has been received.

cc:Mail user agents are very easy to use. It takes only a few minutes to learn the basics of sending and reading e-mail. If cc:Mail has a problem, it is that its user agents are not background programs or desk accessories that pop up and run on top of other programs, but are regular programs. (cc:Mail does have a TSR pop-up program, Messenger, for DOS, which gives you the ability to access, read, and send messages from within other applications. However, Messenger does not have all of the features included in the main mail program.) In the Macintosh environment, you can use MultiFinder to jump from cc:Mail to another application program. If you're a cc:Mail DOS user, however, you have a Notify program that checks the post office in the background at specified intervals. If you receive a new message, you are notified and have the option to suspend the application program, jump into cc:Mail to read the message and create a reply, and then return to the original program.

cc:Mail Remote User Agent Program

cc:Mail has a user agent for people who operate remotely from the LAN. This user agent looks almost identical to the local user agent, but requires a modem so the remote station can dial in to a cc:Mail LAN. Basically, the remote user agent program allows you to create messages offline from the cc:Mail system and to dial in to a local cc:Mail post office to send messages and receive new mail. When the remote user is connected to the post office, all new messages to be read are downloaded from the remote post office, while all messages to be sent are uploaded to the post office. The post office then disconnects, so that the cc:Mail user can read messages while offline, keeping operating costs to a minimum.

Remote users should not be mistaken for e-mail users across a gateway. A remote user is assigned to a cc:Mail post office as if he or she were local. Again, the difference from a local user is that a remote user dials in to the post office via a modem instead of directly accessing the post office on the LAN. cc:Mail's remote user capability has several useful applications:

- Linking a field sales or service force into a cc:Mail post office at the headquarters.

- Allowing local cc:Mail users to access their mail while they are traveling or while they are away from the office.

- Allowing users, such as consultants or other suppliers, to access the cc:Mail post office for temporary periods while local users are doing business with them.

cc:Mail Fax Capabilities

cc:Mail recently took an important step forward in its capabilities by adding the ability to communicate directly to fax machines as if you were sending the message to another cc:Mail system. Users who are not on cc:Mail but must be accessed via a fax machine can be listed directly in cc:Mail's directory and can be intermixed with other cc:Mail users transparently. The only limitation is that cc:Mail cannot send attached computer files to fax machines, but can only send messages created in its text editor or graphics editor (including screen snapshots).

Interestingly, cc:Mail can also receive messages from fax machines. Fax messages are stored as PCX-formatted graphics files, not a mix of text and graphics. This means that you cannot edit or search the "text" of a faxed message. cc:Mail's long-term goal is to handle text and graphics files interchangeably.

Review of the cc:Mail Product Line

At this writing, the cc:Mail product family consists of 17 separate software products, which can be operated together in various configurations. The product family is divided into cc:Mail LAN Packages, cc:Mail Accessories, and cc:Mail External gateways. The manufacturer's suggested retail price is included in parentheses.

cc:Mail LAN Packages

The cc:Mail LAN packages (price listed is per post office) are:

- cc:Mail /DOS Platform Pack, v3.2 (PLP200—$195). This package works on most DOS-based PC LANs. The product consists of one post office server program that can support 25 local mailboxes and associated user agent programs, and an unlimited number of remote mailboxes and associated remote user agent programs.

- cc:Mail Windows Platform Pack, v1.0 (PLP300—$495)

- cc:Mail Macintosh Platform Pack, v1.2 (PLP400—$495). This package is an extension of the cc:Mail LAN package. A cc:Mail for Macintosh software program provides electronic mail for Macintosh users on a Macintosh server. PLP400 is not a stand-alone server product. Instead, it can only operate as part of an overall mail network with at least one cc:Mail LAN package for DOS.

- cc:Mail OS/2 Platform Pack, v1.2 (PLP500—$495). This package is an extension of the cc:Mail LAN package. A cc:Mail for an OS/2 software program provides electronic mail for users on an OS/2 server.

- cc:Mail LAN Package for DOS-French, v3.15 (LAN200-F—$995). This is the same program as PLP200, but in the French language instead of English.

Note that the cc:Mail user agent programs for local users are included as a part of the server product.

cc:Mail Accessories

cc:Mail accessories are products that enhance a basic cc:Mail post office by either expanding the number of users who can be served, or by expanding fundamental capabilities. Accessory products are:

- cc:Mail Automatic Propagation ($995). This product allows for automatic updating among cc:Mail post offices and other mail systems, such as IBM's

PROFS. The updating includes information about users registered in directories, as well as information posted on bulletin boards. The propagation program allows large cc:Mail networks to be managed with a minimal amount of management coordination.

- cc:Mail Expand (EXP200—$595). This package adds an additional 100 cc:Mail mailboxes to one cc:Mail post office.

- cc:Mail Gateway, v3.2 (GTW200—$1,295 per use). This package allows a cc:Mail post office to communicate with remote cc:Mail users and with other e-mail systems, including other cc:Mail post offices and non-cc:Mail post offices. The GTW200 program includes the Message Handling System (MHS) protocol that is used by many LAN-based e-mail systems to exchange messages.

- cc:Mail Remote, v3.2 (RMT200—$295 per machine). This package is the user agent for one remote cc:Mail user who is not on a local LAN. The RMT200 product operates in conjunction with a specific cc:Mail post office.

- cc:Mail Automatic Directory Exchange, v1.0 (ADE200—$995 per post office). ADE200 enables automatic updating of directory information and bulletin boards to multiple cc:Mail post offices and remote users. It requires cc:Mail Gateway.

- cc:Mail Import/Export, v3.2 (IEX200—$995 per server). This package is a toolkit that allows a network administrator to import DOS files into a cc:Mail post office as a cc:Mail message, and to export cc:Mail messages to ASCII DOS files. This product is typically used to communicate with other application programs, so a user can send update information to a database program, or a database program can distribute reports via cc:Mail.

- cc:Mail cc:Fax, v1.2 (FAX200—$1,995 per gateway). This program allows cc:Mail users to send and receive messages created with cc:Mail's editor to fax machines. cc:Fax includes a PC-based fax card and must run on a cc:Mail post office with the GTW200 gateway product.

- cc:Mail FaxView, v1.2 (FXV200—$995 per post office). This program is a subset of the FAX200 program that allows users on one post office to view fax messages. Since a fax card is not included, users cannot receive fax messages directly nor can fax messages be transmitted.

- cc:Mail Network Scheduler II 5-User Pack (SCH205—$395 per post office). This is a calendaring and scheduling package that automatically schedules meetings and shared resources with LAN users. Requires cc:Mail Platform Pack.

- cc:Mail Network Scheduler II 20-User Pack (SCH220—$395 per post office). The pack adds 20 users to one cc:Mail post office. Requires Network Scheduler II 5-User Pack.

- cc:Mail Network Scheduler II Windows Pack (SCH300—$595 per post office). This pack provides scheduling for all Windows users on a post office, up to the number of users for which the pack is purchased. Requires Network Scheduler II 5-User Pack.

cc:Mail External Gateways

The external gateways are programs that allow a cc:Mail post office to communicate with specific e-mail systems. All of these products require a cc:Mail post office running the cc:Mail gateway program. The specific gateway products (price listed is per gateway) are:

- cc:Mail EZlink, v1.0 (EZL200—$695). This program allows users to connect to the EasyLink public e-mail service. The EasyLink service was recently purchased by AT&T. For many years, it was owned and operated by Western Union. An estimated 200,000 EasyLink users send eight million messages per month.

- cc:Mail Link to MCI Mail, v1.0 (MCI200—$1,295). This package allows cc:Mail users to send messages to MCI Mail users and also to use other MCI features, such as telex. MCI Mail is a popular e-mail public service with about 110,000 users who send an estimated two million messages per month.

- cc:Mail PROFSlink, v2.0 (PRF2000—$2,200). This product allows cc:Mail users to exchange messages with IBM's PROFS users. PROFS is an e-mail system that runs on an IBM/VM mainframe. PROFS is one of the leading in-house e-mail systems, with more than two million PROFS users world-wide. The link with PROFS is transparent, so that cc:Mail users and PROFS users can interact as if they were on the same mail system. cc:Mail and PROFS directories can even be updated simultaneously.

- cc:Mail Link to SMTP, v1.2 (SMT200—$2,995). This program allows cc:Mail to exchange messages with users of the Simple Mail Transfer Protocol (SMTP), which is used by the UNIX operating system to exchange messages. The SMTP gateway package opens up a cc:Mail post office to communication with a variety of mail systems, including UNIX mail, The Internet, Bitnet, IBM PROFS, Digital's VMS Mail and All-in-One (via Mailbus), Data General's AOS/VS Mail, and HP DeskMate.

- cc:Mail Link to Soft-Switch, v1.2 (SSW200—$995). This program links cc:Mail to Soft-Switch, an electronic mail interconnection product used by several hundred large corporations to connect a variety of non-compatible e-mail products. Soft-Switch runs on IBM mainframes in conjunction with the SNADS gateway. Companies typically run Soft-Switch when they have several e-mail systems that must be interconnected.

- cc:Mail Telelink, v1.0 (TEL200—$695). This program allows users to exchange messages with US Sprint's SprintMail program. (Formerly, SprintMail was owned by GTE and known as TeleMail.) An estimated 175,000 SprintMail users send an estimated three million messages per month.

- cc:Mail Link to UNIXMail/uucp, v1.0 (UUC200—$695). This program links cc:Mail to UNIX users via the UUCP protocol. This product requires the cc:Mail Import/Export program, not the gateway program.

- cc:Mail Link to X.400. This program links cc:Mail to mail systems that support the X.400 international interconnection standard developed by the International Telephone & Telegraph Consultative Committee (CCITT).

Key cc:Mail Terms and Definitions

The following terms are important to understand:

- Administrator—The person who is responsible for the management of the cc:Mail post office. The administrator assigns user IDs, deletes users from the system, and creates and changes public mail lists and bulletin boards.

- Bulletin Boards—A bulletin board system (BBS) is a public message board with a specific topic name. All users have access to the BBS on a cc:Mail server and can send messages to any BBS. cc:Mail tracks the use of each BBS on a user-by-user basis, so that each user can see the total number of messages in a specific BBS and the number of those messages unread by that user.

- Directory—A list of all users registered in the overall mail system, including both local and remote users, as well as remote systems that can be accessed via gateways. cc:Mail's directory, created and maintained by the cc:Mail administrator, shows whether the user is local or remote.

- Folders—A folder in cc:Mail is the equivalent of a manila file folder. In cc:Mail, individual messages are stored in folders. Each user can have up to 200 folders, and each folder can store 1,600 messages. The folders reside as part of the cc:Mail post office, not as part of the user's own personal computer. cc:Mail, however, not only password-protects the folders, but also encrypts the information, so the folders cannot be read even by the local cc:Mail administrator.

- Gateway—A connecting point between different cc:Mail post offices or electronic mail systems that is created to allow users on multiple systems to send and receive messages as if they were all connected to one post office.

- Inbox (also known as Inbasket)—A specialized folder holding messages that are initially received by a cc:Mail mailbox. The Inbox lists all messages that have been received and not yet been read, as well as all messages that have been read, but not yet filed or deleted.

- Mailbox—In cc:Mail, the mailbox is the equivalent of a user ID, and all of the specific folders associated with that ID, including the Inbox. All users, both local and remote, must be assigned mailboxes.

- Message—A message is the basic unit of communications in cc:Mail. A message consists of the envelope information in the message header, and the message items inside the envelope. The header information includes administrative information about the message, such as sender and recipient(s), while the items contain the information to be communicated.

- Message Items—In cc:Mail, a message item is the information that is to be communicated within a message between sender and receiver(s). A message can have four types of items—text, fax, graphics, and attached files. In a single message, you can have up to 20 separate items in any combination. Text items are created using cc:Mail's text editor, but can be created with any text editor, and can be up to 20,000 characters. Graphics items are usually created using cc:Mail's graphics editor or screen snapshot program, and can contain one screen of graphics. An attached file can be one data or application file of an unlimited length. A fax item is a monochrome PCX file that can be created by a PCX editor or scanner, or faxed into cc:Mail.

- Message Receipts—In cc:Mail, a sender can request that a message be sent "certified," meaning cc:Mail will send a notification to the sender specifying the time and date when the recipient(s) read the message.

- Post Office—The cc:Mail database that resides on a central server and contains all of the mailboxes for individual recipients.

- X.400—An international communications standard created to allow different electronic mail systems to exchange messages. While not every mail system uses X.400 to communicate, the existence of the standard has focused attention on the need to exchange messages, and has resulted in a variety of proprietary gateways that perform the same function with greater effectiveness and efficiency than X.400.

cc:Mail for PCs

USING CC: MAIL

CHAPTER 3

Loading and Running cc:Mail for PCs

This section discusses cc:Mail on the IBM PC and compatibles, using version 3.2. If you are using an older version some of the parameters may have changed slightly, but the basics will be the same.

Requirements

You can run cc:Mail on an XT-class machine, but cc:Mail runs much faster on a 286 or higher machine. You'll need 320 kilobytes of memory and DOS version 3.1 or higher. Of course, you'll also have to be operating on a local area network (LAN). If you have any questions about your PC's configuration, ask your cc:Mail administrator. cc:Mail's graphics editor can be used without a mouse, but it is very cumbersome. If you use this feature a great deal, you may find you need a mouse.

Loading cc:Mail

Before running cc:Mail, you must be registered at the server (the local cc:Mail post office). Your cc:Mail administrator creates your account and registers you with a name and password. If you do not know or have forgotten your cc:Mail name or password, contact your cc:Mail administrator.

To run cc:Mail, you must log on to the LAN, because the cc:Mail program is stored on the LAN server. The user portion of the program is loaded into your PC from the LAN. While the user program runs on your PC, all of the data is accessed across the LAN on the server.

To run cc:Mail, you can either invoke the mail program and then enter your user name and password when prompted, or you can enter all of this information in a single command. Here is a sample, assuming that your local PC is disk C:

```
C> F:MAIL JOHN JONES TWQOP G:
```

The F:MAIL designates that the MAIL command be issued on the F: drive. This means that the cc:Mail program itself is stored in drive F:, which is located at the server. If cc:Mail was in a subdirectory on the F: drive, the command might look like this:

```
C> F:\CCMAIL\MAIL.
```

"JOHN JONES" is the user's name, and was assigned by the cc:Mail administrator. It must be spelled exactly as provided, but cc:Mail user names are not case-sensitive, so "John Jones" and "john jones" are equivalent.

TWQOP is the password in this sample case. It must be typed exactly as spelled, but it is not case-sensitive. The first time you use cc:Mail, you should change your password. Use the command under the "**M**anage mailbox" command at the Main Menu. When choosing a password, pick something you'll remember, but don't choose something too obvious.

The last part of the sample login is the directory containing the cc:Mail database, which is drive G: in the example. This is supplied by your cc:Mail administrator. If you typed in F:MAIL M:, you could have also accessed cc:Mail, had the cc:Mail database been the M: drive. You would have been prompted for your name and password before being allowed to enter the program.

Other Command-Line Options

There are several other options that you can set when you log on to cc:Mail. Enter these commands at the end of the command line in any order. You may be instructed by your cc:Mail administrator to enter one or more of the following commands:

ARCHIVE/path

This defines the location of the user's archive files. If this option is not defined, cc:Mail assumes that archive files are stored in the same directory from which the user started cc:Mail. For example, if you started up cc:Mail while in the root directory of the C: drive, any time you gave a command to save a message as an archived file, the message would be stored in the C: root directory.

MONO

This tells cc:Mail you are using a monochrome monitor with a color graphics card. If this is not set, cc:Mail assumes you are using a color monitor.

FIFO

This tells cc:Mail to display the oldest messages in your Inbox first ("First In/First Out"). If not invoked, cc:Mail will list the newest messages first.

FILES/path

This command defines the pathway to access files associated with DOS operations. If this option is not defined, cc:Mail assumes that files are stored in the same directory from which you started cc:Mail. Do not confuse this with the directory in which cc:Mail stores your mail folders. Mail folders are stored on the server in the same directory as the cc:Mail database, which is already defined in a command line option. Unless instructed by your cc:Mail administrator, do not use this option.

KEYS/[abc]

This runs a set of power-user commands when cc:Mail starts up. The commands are defined by what is typed after the slash. For example, if you always want to see your Inbox immediately upon logging on, you would type KEYS/r, which is the power-user command for "**R**ead inbox messages."

LPTx

This specifies the printer port used by cc:Mail. The default is LPT1. Use this only if you have more than one printer and want to use a printer defined other than LPT1. You may also use this to override the regular printer for a specific cc:Mail session.

MOUSE

This tells cc:Mail that you have a mouse set up for operation. cc:Mail allows you to use the mouse when editing graphics or when invoking menu commands.

REENTER

This command gives you the "Name:" and "Password:" prompts after you have finished a cc:Mail session. This allows you to reenter cc:Mail after exiting without running the cc:Mail command again. It is only of value if you have more than one user ID. In general, this command is for those who are signing on to check the mail for several people.

Creating Command Batch Files

cc:Mail gives you a lot of options for signing on. However, once you've decided which options you want, you'll usually enter the same login command every time. At that point, you should turn your login command into a batch file. A DOS batch file is a text file containing a series of commands that can be executed from DOS. Its name always ends with the 3-letter extension .BAT. Most PC users know about the AUTOEXEC.BAT file, a batch file that executes when you turn your PC on.

If you have a complex command sequence, create a batch file that runs the command. Here is an example. Let's say you have to use this command to access cc:Mail:

F:\ccMAIL\MAIL H. JOHNSON M: MOUSE LPT2

Instead of having to type this every time you want to access cc:Mail (which is enough to discourage anyone from using the program), create a batch file, such as MAIL.BAT, that has this command. Here's how to create the batch file:

```
C>copy con mail.bat

F:\ccMAIL\MAIL H. JOHNSON  M: MOUSE LPT2

^Z
```

You can press F6 to type the CTRL-Z that ends the batch file. Once ended, you can invoke the batch file in the directory in which it is stored. If the directory is defined in the DOS PATH command in your AUTOEXEC.BAT file, then you can type the command while in any directory. For more information on batch files, contact your cc:Mail administrator.

A Word About Your Password

Take your password seriously. E-mail does not have the same security that a desk has. Someone must be physically at your desk to read your files, but the same is not true of your e-mail files. They can be accessed by anyone from any workstation. Therefore, you should not create a command line that has your password in it, even though cc:Mail gives you that option. Doing so would give anyone the ability to sign on to cc:Mail as if they were you. Leave your password out of any command-line batch file you create. cc:Mail will prompt you for it before logging you into the program.

Logging on to cc:Mail

After you have entered cc:Mail by running the command line, you are placed in cc:Mail's Main Menu, as shown below.

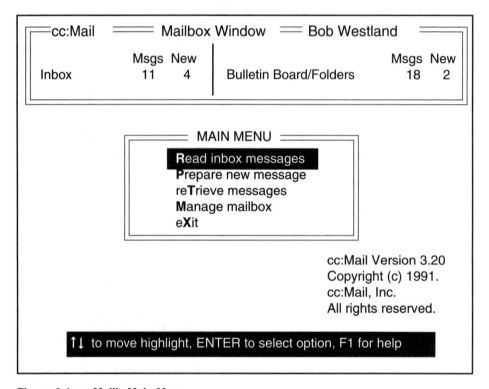

Figure 3-1. cc:Mail's Main Menu

cc:Mail's Main Menu gives you access to its four main functions: reading your mail, preparing new messages, retrieving past messages, and managing your mailbox. Most of your time will be spent performing the specific functions, not in the Main Menu. Main Menu commands have these broad functions:

- "**R**ead inbox messages" lets you read the mail stored in your Inbox— typically new messages sent to you, or messages you have not yet deleted.

- "**P**repare new messages" lets you create messages to send to other mail users.

- "re**T**rieve messages" lets you read messages stored in your mail folders that reside at the post office, stored in bulletin boards, or stored in private archives on your PC.

- "**M**anage mailbox" lets you create or change mailing lists and folders. It also lets you view the directory and change your password.

- "e**X**it" gets you out of cc:Mail and back into DOS.

To invoke these commands move the **Up** and **Down** cursor keys to the command you want and press **ENTER**. To go directly to a particular command, press the highlighted, capitalized letter of the command, such as T to select the "re**T**rieve messages" command.

cc:Mail menus are layered, and each menu choice leads to submenus if required. Only available options are displayed, so if you cannot invoke a command at a specific point in the program, you will not be offered the command option.

Information in the Main Menu

The Mailbox window at the top of the screen is divided into two sections that show how many messages are stored in your Inbox and bulletin boards/folders, and how many of these messages are new. As messages are read, stored, and deleted, the window is updated.

A menu bar with up/down arrow keys is at the bottom of the window and says:

↑↓ to move highlight, ENTER to select option, F1 for help

Figure 3-2. Menu bar showing how to invoke specific commands

The bar is a reminder of what you can do to invoke specific commands. Use the **Up** and **Down** cursor keys to select a command and the **ENTER** key to invoke the command. At any time, press the **F1** key for the Help files.

Important cc:Mail Command Keys

You should know about the following important command keys:

Alt-1/Snapshot

This key sequence (press **Alt** and **1** at the same time) brings up cc:Mail's unique Snapshot feature, which takes a picture of the screen within any application and allows it to be saved as a file that can be sent by cc:Mail. Snapshot capability is only available when the TSR SNAPSHOT.COM has been loaded into memory.

Alt-2/New Messages?

This key sequence (press **Alt** and **2** at the same time) runs the cc:Mail Messenger or Notify program, depending upon which program you are using. MESSENGR.EXE allows you to read mail, prepare text messages, and reply to messages while in another application. NOTIFY.COM is an older cc:Mail program that notifies you when you have a new message and lets you see the header of the message while in another application program.

Alt-F1/Highlight

This key sequence (press **Alt** and **F1** at the same time) brings up the Highlight Menu while you are using the text editor. The Highlight Menu allows you to change the text and background colors of specific areas of your message to distinguish them from the rest of the message.

Cursor and Movement Keys

The cursor and movement keys on the numeric pad are important for maneuvering around cc:Mail to select commands. The **Up** and **Down** arrow keys (**8** and **2** on the pad) are used to highlight commands, while the **Home**, **Pg Up**, **Pg Dn**, and **End** keys (**7**, **9**, **3**, and **1**, respectively) are used to move to the corresponding corners of a menu.

ENTER

The **ENTER** key is also called the **RETURN** key. Pressing this key will execute the command that is highlighted by the cursor.

ESC

The **ESC** or escape key is used to cancel a command or menu. Pressing **ESC** will clear what you were doing and take you back to the previous command or menu.

F1/Help

The **F1** key is used in cc:Mail to access the Help Menu. cc:Mail provides online help with every command. While online help does not always offer enough detail, you should give it a try before referring to this book or the cc:Mail manual.

F9/DOS

From any menu, the F9 key will load a DOS command shell. Type **EXIT** from DOS to return to cc:Mail.

Power User Keys

Most cc:Mail menu commands can be executed using its "power user key," a single letter that can invoke a command directly. Once you become familiar with cc:Mail, you can type multiple power user keys without waiting to read the menus.

cc:Mail's Main Menu Functions

cc:Mail's Main Menu functions (Read mail, prepare mail, access files, or manage mail operations) each have certain well-defined usage patterns that repeat themselves as you become more familiar with them. cc:Mail's functions are determined by the options that are available from the menus and by commands that are available at each stage.

cc:Mail's main usage patterns are:

- Reading and replying to incoming messages.

- Preparing and sending new messages.

- Reviewing stored messages.

- Managing your mailbox.

Reading and Replying to Messages

When you choose "Read inbox messages" from the Main Menu, you will be allowed to select messages from the Inbox. Once the messages are selected and/or read, you will see the Action Menu, where you will be able to reply, forward, copy, move, or delete messages. Replying and forwarding takes you to the Send Menu to create the message, attach files, add addresses, and review the message items. While in the Send Menu, you cycle among the Address and Attach Menus as required to create addresses and attach items.

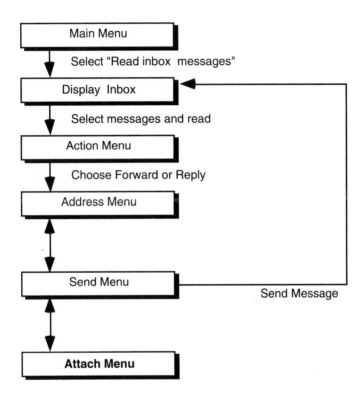

Figure 3-3. Reading and replying to a cc:Mail message

Preparing and Sending Messages

Preparing and sending messages uses four menus. The Address Menu lets you select individuals, bulletin boards, and/or folders to receive messages, and also lets you set the priority of the message and request return receipts.

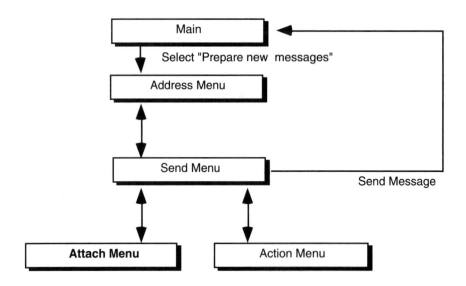

Figure 3-4. Preparing and sending cc:Mail messages

The Send Menu lets you create and send messages. It cycles you among the Address, Attach, and Action Menus, letting you select addresses, attach DOS files or other items, and review and edit your messages.

Reviewing Stored Messages

When reviewing your stored messages, you will spend most of your time cycling between the Retrieve Menu (which allows you to select messages stored in your folder or on public bulletin boards) and the Action Menu (which lets you delete, move, or copy these messages). You can also edit the messages and resend them. However, once you select a message, you'll return to the Send Menu and its options.

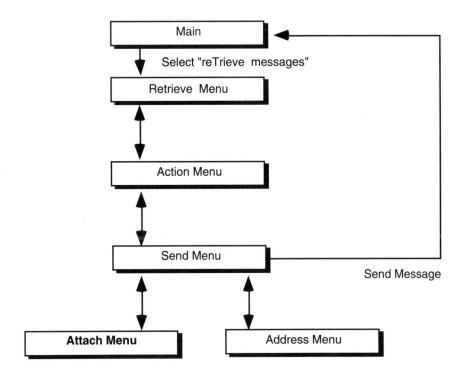

Figure 3-5. Reviewing stored messages

Managing Your Mailbox

The management cycle allows you to delete or change the name of folders; to delete, edit, or change the name of your mailing list; to view public mail lists and the main directory; and to change your cc:Mail profile, including your password, printer type, and printer port.

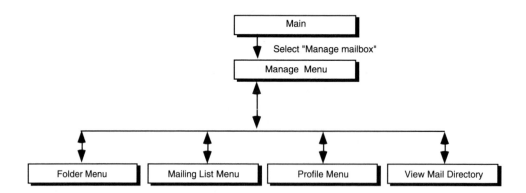

Figure 3-6. Managing your mailbox

Circular Flow of cc:Mail

cc:Mail cycles you between menus that perform specific tasks. The main messaging menus are Send, Address, Action, and Attach. Messages are created, reviewed, and stored using these menus. Remember: cc:Mail's menus will present you with only active choices.

CHAPTER 4

Reading Messages on PCs

Handling a Sample Message

Reading messages in cc:Mail or any e-mail system is like reading messages in the inbox on your desk. Imagine you just sat down at your desk and pulled the top memo from your inbox. It's a memo to you from your boss:

> We will have a staff meeting next Wednesday at 9 a.m. in conference room 101. Please let me know if you have any conflict in attending and also notify your staff that they should either attend or let my secretary know if they cannot attend.

You would probably have copies made for your staff members and send the original back to your boss with a reply saying whether or not you can attend. All e-mail systems are set up to perform these tasks as efficiently as possible. With an e-mail system, you can accomplish with a few simple commands on the computer what it might take several sheets of paper and trips to the copy machine to accomplish in paper form.

Step 1: Reading the message

When you first log on to cc:Mail, you will see a Status Window that shows you how many messages you have and how many are new. The Main Menu appears in a window in the middle of the screen. The top option, "Read inbox messages," is highlighted. Press **ENTER** to execute the command.

Next you see a list of messages in your Inbox. The most recent messages are at the top and unread messages are in bold. Move the cursor to the message you want to read and press **ENTER**. You will see the text of the message.

Step 2: Replying to the message

Press **ENTER** while you are reading the message. The message will be replaced by a summary of its contents and an Action Menu will pop up in the middle of the screen. Highlight the command "repl**Y** to message" with the cursor and press **EN-TER**. Type your reply in the field that appears and press **F10** when you are finished. When the Send Menu appears, the command "Send message" is already highlighted. Press **ENTER** to send the reply and you will return to the Inbox.

Step 3: Forwarding the message

Select the message in your Inbox and press **ENTER**. Once you have read the message, press **ENTER**. The message will be replaced by a summary of its contents and an Action Menu will pop up in the middle of the screen. Highlight the command "Forward the message" with the cursor and press **ENTER**.

The Address Window will appear. Scroll to the name of each person you want to forward the message to and press **ENTER**. The names will be added to the list. When you are finished, press **Esc**, and then select "e**N**d addressing" by pressing **ENTER** and "Send message" by pressing **ENTER** again. You have forwarded the message and will be returned to the Inbox.

That's all there is to using cc:Mail for most tasks. Notice how often cc:Mail defaults to what you need to do and you only have to press **ENTER** to execute the command. This chapter will look at each of these steps in more depth and show you some options for using cc:Mail more effectively.

Opening the Inbox

When you first log on to cc:Mail, you are placed in the Main Menu:

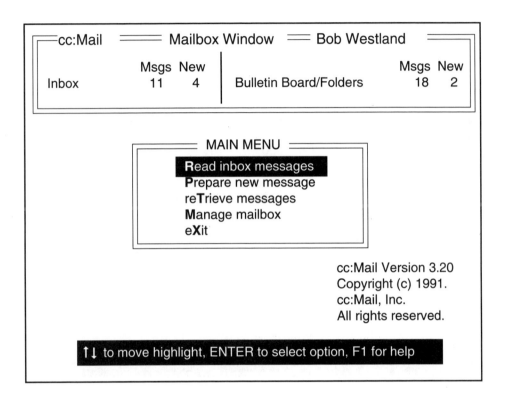

Figure 4-1. The cc:Mail Main Menu

You read new messages by selecting the "**R**ead inbox messages" command from the Main Menu. This option is available only if you have messages in your Inbox. Messages are listed in the Inbox, along with the following information:

- Sender's name

- Date sent

- Size of the message in bytes

- Type of message (t = text, f = file, g = graphics, x = fax)

- First 34 characters of the subject of the message

```
Inbox
 11   Ronald Adler      8/5/91   110t     Need for meeting
 10   Carlos Castillo   8/5/91   7146tgf  new product outline
  9   Jerry Littler     8/5/91   600tg    Earnings report
  8   Abigail Fraser    8/5/91   240t     A Question?
  7   Raymond Bolton    8/4/91   8000tgf  Consulting proposal
  6   Jerry Littler     8/4/91   350t     report on meeting w/ Johnson
  5   Ronald Adler      8/4/91   800t     prelim report - Williams meet
  4   Carlos Castillos  8/3/91   2400tf   wp file for editing
  3   Abigail Fraser    8/3/91   1500t    observations
  2   Raymond Bolton    8/3/91   1200t    questions on consulting work
  1   Raymond Bolton    8/3/91   700t     reply to your query




 ↑↓ and ENTER to display message, F5 and F6 to select, Esc to end
```

Figure 4-2. A cc:Mail Inbox listing

Messages you have not read appear in bold. Messages are stored chronologically, with the most recent message at the top. This order can be changed using the FIFO command when you run cc:Mail.

Reading Messages

There are three ways to open messages. You can open a single message by using the **up** and **down** arrow keys to highlight a single message and pressing ENTER. You can select multiple messages in two ways: you can use the up and down arrow keys to highlight messages and press **F5** to select individual messages, or you can press **F5** to select the beginning of a block and **F6** to select its end. Once you have selected the messages you want to read, press **ENTER**.

Fax messages can be sent to cc:Mail users with the cc:Fax optional program. A fax is saved in graphics format and can be displayed on your screen and/or printed out.

When a message is selected, it pops up in a separate window. At the top is the message number in parentheses, the sender's name, the date and time the message was sent, and the number of characters and lines in the text items, plus the number of files attached, if any.

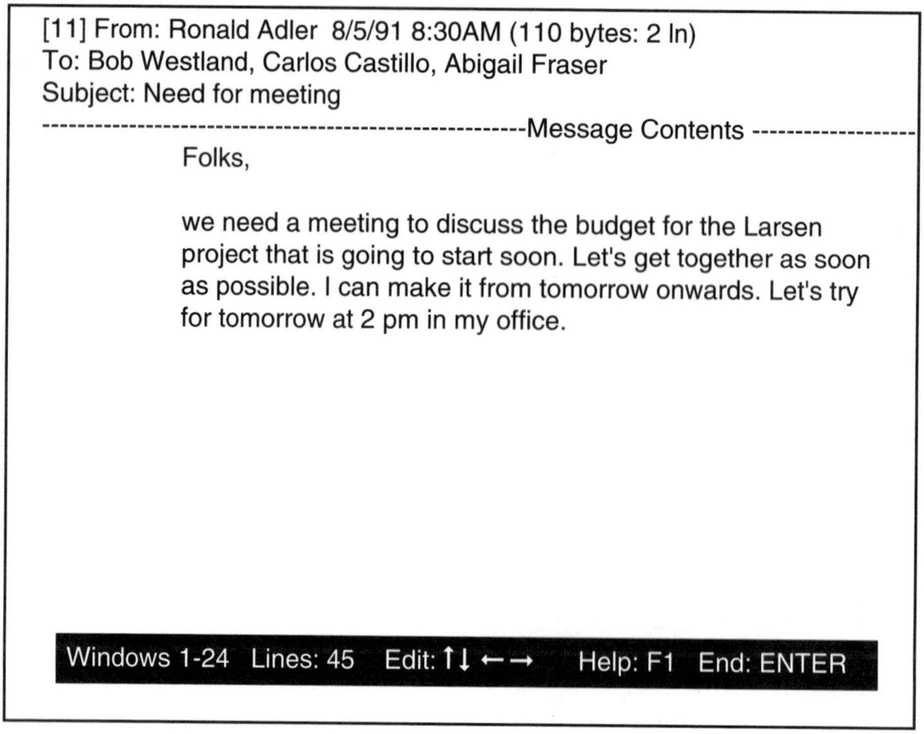

```
[11] From: Ronald Adler  8/5/91 8:30AM (110 bytes: 2 ln)
To: Bob Westland, Carlos Castillo, Abigail Fraser
Subject: Need for meeting
---------------------------------------------------------Message Contents ------------------
        Folks,

        we need a meeting to discuss the budget for the Larsen
        project that is going to start soon. Let's get together as soon
        as possible. I can make it from tomorrow onwards. Let's try
        for tomorrow at 2 pm in my office.




        Windows 1-24  Lines: 45   Edit: ↑↓ ←→     Help: F1  End: ENTER
```

Figure 4-3. A cc:Mail message

Using the Action Menu to Handle Messages

After reading the message, press the **ENTER** key. The message disappears, cc:Mail's Action Menu pops up over the message, and the Status Window reappears at the top of the screen. The message you have just read is no longer listed as New in the Status Window. The Action Menu appears as shown in Figure 4-4.

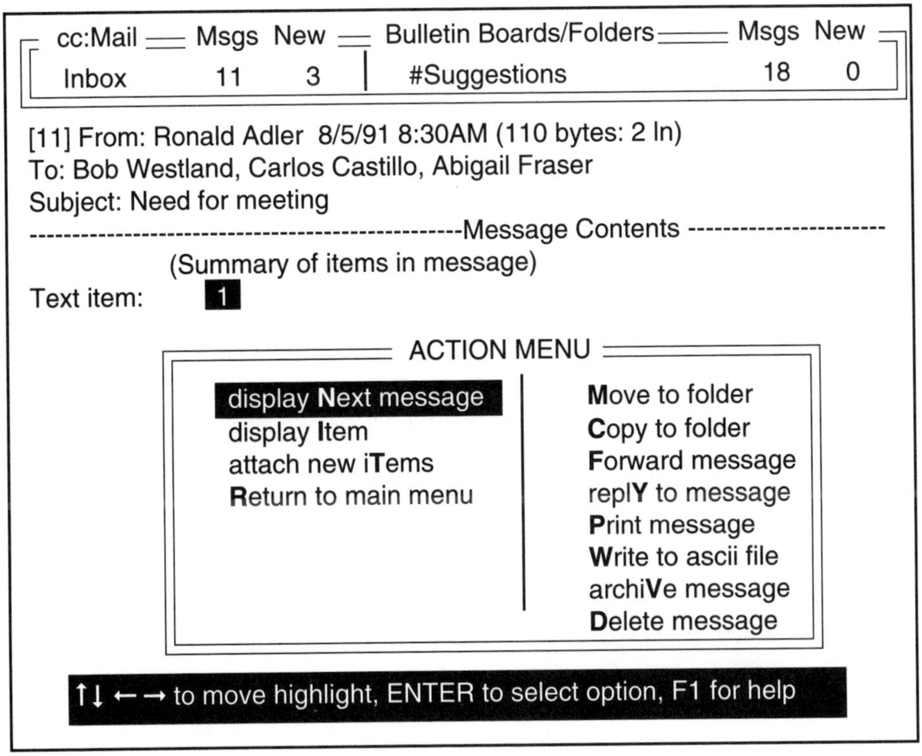

```
┌─ cc:Mail ── Msgs  New ── Bulletin Boards/Folders ── Msgs  New ─┐
│  Inbox        11    3   │ #Suggestions              18    0    │
└────────────────────────────────────────────────────────────────┘
```

[11] From: Ronald Adler 8/5/91 8:30AM (110 bytes: 2 ln)
To: Bob Westland, Carlos Castillo, Abigail Fraser
Subject: Need for meeting
---Message Contents -----------------------
                    (Summary of items in message)
Text item: ▐1▌

```
┌──────────────────── ACTION MENU ─────────────────────┐
│   ┌─────────────────────────┐                          │
│   │ display Next message    │   Move to folder         │
│     display Item            │   Copy to folder         │
│     attach new iTems        │   Forward message        │
│     Return to main menu     │   replY to message       │
│                             │   Print message          │
│                             │   Write to ascii file    │
│                             │   archiVe message        │
│                             │   Delete message         │
└──────────────────────────────────────────────────────┘
```

↑↓ ←→ to move highlight, ENTER to select option, F1 for help

Figure 4-4. The cc:Mail Action Menu

The Action Menu lists every command that you can execute after reading the message. The first command, "display **N**ext message," is highlighted. The menu bar at the bottom of the screen now includes the **Left** and **Right** arrow keys as well. Use these keys to move the cursor between the left and right sides of the Action Menu. You may also press the highlighted, capitalized letter to invoke a command.

At this point, you can do any one of the listed commands, or, if you choose, perform any number of these commands in sequence. This is an important point. When you take an action in cc:Mail, such as replying to a message, you are returned to the Action Menu, not to the Main Menu, after the command is completed, so that you can perform further actions on the message. When you are finished acting on the message, you must select "**R**eturn to main menu" to leave the Inbox and perform some other function.

Replying to Messages

Creating and Sending a Reply

If you wish to reply to the message after reading it, select the "repl**Y** to message" command from the Action Menu. A message header is created with your name at the top, the name of the sender of the message is displayed in the To: field, and the subject of the original message is in the subject field. You are placed in cc:Mail's editor to create a reply. Type in the reply as if you were working in a word processor. Words will wrap around at the end of a line. (Refer to Appendix A for more information on using the editor.)

When you are finished typing your reply, press F10. The text disappears and is replaced with a summary of items in the message, which shows just a single text item. The Send Menu then pops up as shown in Figure 4-5.

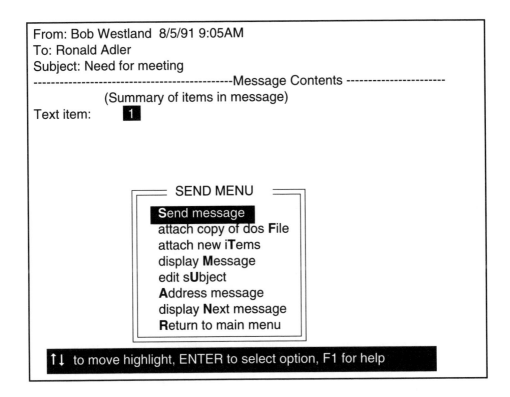

Figure 4-5. The cc:Mail Send Menu

If you're finished, press **ENTER** or **S** to execute the highlighted "Send message" command. The Send Menu also lists other options that include attaching files, editing the message or address, or cancelling the message by returning to the Main Menu. (See Chapter 5 for more information on the Send Menu.)

Adding a Reply to the Original Message

Sometimes you'll reply to a paper memo by writing your answer at the bottom and returning it to the sender. cc:Mail has a similar function. You can type your reply on the original message and send the edited message back to the sender.

When should you use this function and when should you use the "replY to message" command? Including the original message in your reply reminds everyone of the context of your reply. Since cc:Mail saves the original message, the original unedited message is still available to you. If the amount of available storage on your cc:Mail server is an issue, keep your replies short. If storage isn't an issue, send the original with the reply.

To send a reply in this fashion, don't press **ENTER** right after reading the message. While you are reading, the menu bar has these commands:

```
Window 1-24   Lines: 45      Edit: ↑↓ ← →   Help: F1    End: ENTER
```

Figure 4-6. The cc:Mail Edit Window menu bar

While it may not be immediately apparent, the **Up**, **Down**, **Left**, and **Right** cursor keys are active. If you press the cursor keys before pressing the **ENTER** key, you can add anything you want to the message, or even change the message itself. Please note that you cannot send the message as if it were sent by someone else; all changes you make can only be sent out under your name.

To reply to the message, move to the desired location in the message using the cursor keys. If there are more than 24 lines, use the **PgUp** and **PgDn** keys to scroll the message. If necessary, press the **Insert** key to change the editing mode from Overwrite to Insert.

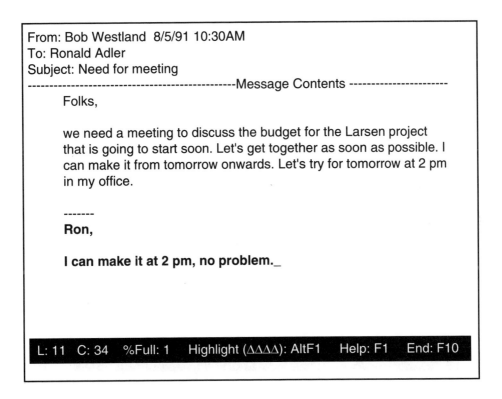

From: Bob Westland 8/5/91 10:30AM
To: Ronald Adler
Subject: Need for meeting
---Message Contents ----------------------
   Folks,

   we need a meeting to discuss the budget for the Larsen project
   that is going to start soon. Let's get together as soon as possible. I
   can make it from tomorrow onwards. Let's try for tomorrow at 2 pm
   in my office.

   Ron,

   I can make it at 2 pm, no problem._

L: 11   C: 34   %Full: 1   Highlight (△△△△): AltF1   Help: F1   End: F10

Figure 4-7. Replying to an original message

The reply is shown in bold in Figure 4.7. In normal cc:Mail use, the reply is displayed in regular type. Keep in mind that if you use this method of sending a reply, cc:Mail does not know you want to reply. When you have finished editing the message, press F10 (**ENTER** is now an editing command to begin a new paragraph). You will see the Address Menu:

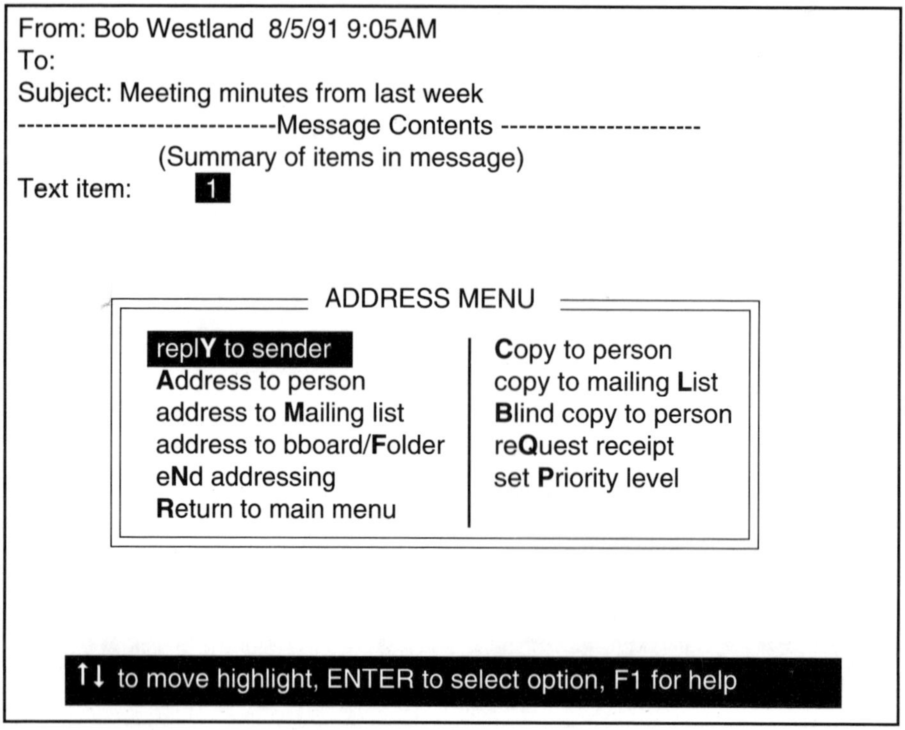

From: Bob Westland 8/5/91 9:05AM
To:
Subject: Meeting minutes from last week
----------------------------Message Contents ----------------------
                    (Summary of items in message)
Text item: ▮1▮

======================= ADDRESS MENU =======================

replY to sender   Copy to person
Address to person   copy to mailing List
address to Mailing list   Blind copy to person
address to bboard/Folder   reQuest receipt
eNd addressing   set Priority level
Return to main menu

↑↓ to move highlight, ENTER to select option, F1 for help

Figure 4-8. The cc:Mail Address Menu

The Address Menu is the same as that shown when sending a new message, with the exception that it has the "replY to sender" command. Select the "replY to sender" command to select the sender as the addressee. (For information on the other commands, see Chapter 5.) If the message has been sent to other users, you will be asked if you want to send your reply to the other addressees. Otherwise, once you select the "replY to sender" command, the Address Menu changes to read:

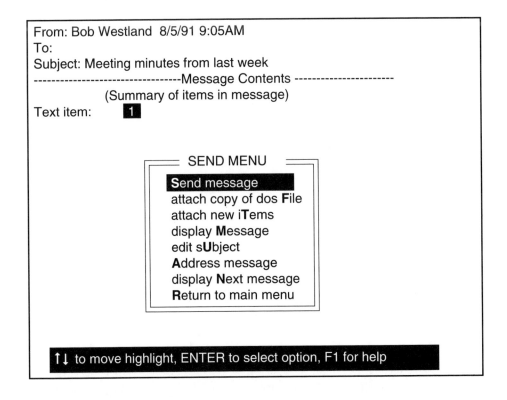

Figure 4-9. The Address Menu after the "replY to sender" command is invoked

Invoke the "eNd addressing" command, and the Send Menu pops up as follows:

```
┌──────────────────────────────────────────────────────────┐
│ From: Bob Westland  8/5/91 9:05AM                          │
│ To:                                                        │
│ Subject: Meeting minutes from last week                    │
│ ----------------------------------Message Contents -----------------------│
│            (Summary of items in message)                   │
│ Text item:       █1█                                       │
│                                                            │
│              ┌═══════ SEND MENU ═══════┐                   │
│              │ ██Send message██         │                  │
│              │ attach copy of dos File  │                  │
│              │ attach new iTems         │                  │
│              │ display Message          │                  │
│              │ edit sUbject             │                  │
│              │ Address message          │                  │
│              │ display Next message     │                  │
│              │ Return to main menu      │                  │
│              └──────────────────────────┘                  │
│                                                            │
│ ██↑↓ to move highlight, ENTER to select option, F1 for help██│
└──────────────────────────────────────────────────────────┘
```

Figure 4-10. The Send Menu after the "eNd addressing" command is invoked

Select "Send message" to send the reply. Although it requires the additional step of addressing the reply to the original sender, this is a rapid way to reply to messages.

You can instantly reply to a message (if there are no additional addressees) by typing in the reply, pressing **F10** to exit and then pressing **ENTER** three times to execute the default commands.

Forwarding Messages

You may want to share a message with people to whom it was not originally addressed. One way is to add their names to the address list of your edited reply.

To forward the message as originally sent after reading the message, press **ENTER**, and select "Forward message". Do not modify the original message if you wish to show the original author, because you will be listed as the author of a modified message. If you respond to a message by adding your own reply without entering the editor, you can forward that message. See the discussion above about the two ways of replying to a message.

Selecting the "Forward message" command places you in the Address Directory, where you select an address. (See the section on addressing messages in Chapter 5 for detailed information on using the directory.) After you select the addresses of the people to whom you wish to forward the message, cc:Mail adds a new message header, above the original message header, with your name as the sender. The two headings are separated with a dashed line.

You can edit the message before you send it. Select the "display Message" command from the Send Menu, and edit the message as you would any other message you are sending. Normally, the dashed line separating the messages will have the word "Forwarded" to show where the original message begins. If you edit the text of the original message at this point, the words "Forwarded with Changes" will appear on the dashed line.

Moving, Copying, Deleting, and Archiving Messages

After acting on the message by replying or forwarding it, you can then move, copy, delete, or archive the message to a DOS file. You can move the message in one of the folders you have created at the cc:Mail post office, or you can place copies in one or more folders. You may also create a new folder on the fly. (Chapter 6, Managing Stored Messages, describes these steps in detail.) Moving the message automatically eliminates the message from your Inbox, while copying the message allows it to remain in your Inbox. Deleting the message removes it from your Inbox. Archiving the message stores it on a floppy, network drive, or local hard drive.

Why archive messages? First, if your cc:Mail post office is crowded with lots of users and messages, you lower the risk of running out of disk space. Second, when you archive messages, they can be stored on floppy disks and locked away in a safe or another secure place. In short, while cc:Mail provides password security, archiving can provide physical security.

However, there are some reasons not to archive messages. When a message is at the cc:Mail post office server, you can always resend it. When the message is archived it must be retrieved from the archive by cc:Mail in order to be used as a message. Also, cc:Mail encrypts all of its messages, which is typically more secure than files stored on local PCs.

Printing and Writing Messages to ASCII Files

Finally, you have two options for saving messages outside of cc:Mail. You can print them or save them to an ASCII text file that can be read by most other applications. Select "**P**rint messages" to print selected messages to your printer. The default is LPT1 unless you specified a different printer in your command line when you ran cc:Mail from DOS. (See Chapter 3 for information on the LPT command line option.) If you want to print to some other port once you have entered cc:Mail, you can use the "**W**rite to ascii file" command and name the file LPTx or COMx, where "x" is the port number.

Writing the message to an ASCII file allows you to load the information into a word processor or to send it using another mail system that does not interconnect to cc:Mail. When you select the "**W**rite to ascii file" command, you will be shown a list of files in the current directory and asked to name the file. Be sure to give the file a name that is already in use, unless you want to overwrite the existing file. cc:Mail will create an ASCII file that contains the text of your message.

Detaching an attached PC file

If you receive a PC file attached to a message, you will see the "cOpy item to dos file" command in the Action Menu. Invoke this command to detach a file that has been attached by another sender. When you invoke the command, you will be asked to name the DOS file.

Summary—Managing your Inbox

Reading messages in cc:Mail is very simple. If you have any questions about the process, think about what you might do if you were dealing with a paper memo. Also keep in mind that you must manage your Inbox on cc:Mail just as you must manage your regular mailbox. Both can get cluttered. Do not be afraid to use the Move, Archive, Print, and Delete commands—especially Delete. The hard disk at the cc:Mail post office and your own hard disk are limited resources. Many e-mail users, particularly new ones, store everything and then forget about it until their disk fills up. Working this way with cc:Mail will clog up the hard disk at your mail server, limiting available storage and causing you to add more expensive hardware.

CHAPTER 5

Creating and Sending Messages

Sending a cc:Mail message is simple. cc:Mail has options for creating text, graphics, and formatted messages. You can send messages to users at your local post office, and your cc:Mail system can be set up to send messages to users on other cc:Mail systems, to users on many other non-cc:Mail e-mail systems, and to fax machines. In some cases, you may be limited to sending only text messages or text and graphics messages. Check with your cc:Mail administrator for restrictions. In general, however, if your PC supports graphics and you have cc:Fax, you will probably be able to create graphics and fax items whenever you wish.

Sending a Sample Message

Step 1: Addressing the message

Let's send a sample message with an attached file to see how simple it is. If you are not already in the Main Menu, select "**R**eturn to main menu" from your current menu. Select "**P**repare new message" from the Main Menu, and "**A**ddress to person" from the Address Menu.

A good way to send a sample message is to address it to yourself. Type the first few letters of your name until it is highlighted in the address window and press **ENTER**. Your name will be added to the "To" field of the message. Press **F10** or **Esc** to finish adding names, and press **ENTER** to "e**N**d addressing" from the Address Menu.

Step 2: Creating and sending the message

Type the subject of the message in the subject field and press **ENTER**. Type your message in the message field. Press **F10** when you are finished editing your message, and the Action Menu will appear. You can use this menu to edit the message, subject, or addressees. You can attach other files to your message, or simply press **ENTER** to execute the "Send message" command.

This chapter will explore the process of creating and sending messages in greater depth, including a section on attaching files to your message.

Starting a New Message

Creating and sending messages is done with the second function on the Main Menu, "**Prepare new message**":

Figure 5-1. The Prepare new message command in the Main Menu

cc:Mail opens up a screen that allows you to create a message, as follows:

```
From: Bob Westland  8/5/91 9:40AM
To:
Subject:
---------------------------------Message Contents -----------------------
None




                    ════ ADDRESS MENU ════
         ┌─────────────────────────┬───────────────────────┐
         │ Address to person       │ Copy to person        │
         │ address to Mailing list │ copy to mailing List  │
         │ address to bboard/Folder│ Blind copy to person  │
         │ eNd addressing          │ set Priority level    │
         │ Return to main menu     │ reQuest receipt       │
         └─────────────────────────┴───────────────────────┘



    ↑↓ ←→  to move highlight, ENTER to select option, F1 for help
```

Figure 5-2. Screen in which a message is created

The screen has your name at the top in the From: field, along with To: and Subject: fields that are empty. The Address Menu is in the center of the screen.

Addressing the Message

To address the message, you must first determine whether you want to send the message to a person, mailing list, bulletin board, or folder. Select the appropriate command by moving the cursor and pressing **ENTER**. When you are finished, choose "eNd addressing." (You may end addressing before you address the message, and return to the Address Menu later.) The cursor will be placed in the "Subject" field.

Addressing to Individuals

When you select the "**A**ddress to person" command, a screen pops up with cc:Mail's directory of users:

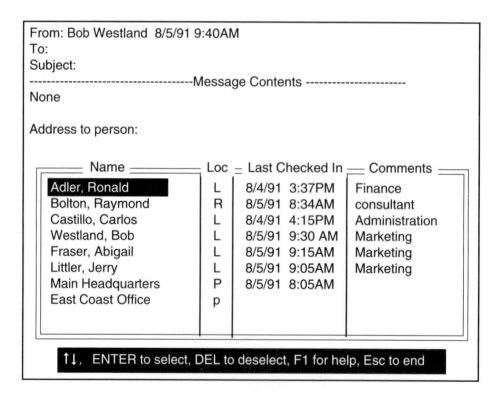

From: Bob Westland 8/5/91 9:40AM
To:
Subject:
-------------------------------------Message Contents ----------------------
None

Address to person:

Name	Loc	Last Checked In	Comments
Adler, Ronald	L	8/4/91 3:37PM	Finance
Bolton, Raymond	R	8/5/91 8:34AM	consultant
Castillo, Carlos	L	8/4/91 4:15PM	Administration
Westland, Bob	L	8/5/91 9:30 AM	Marketing
Fraser, Abigail	L	8/5/91 9:15AM	Marketing
Littler, Jerry	L	8/5/91 9:05AM	Marketing
Main Headquarters	P	8/5/91 8:05AM	
East Coast Office	p		

↑↓, ENTER to select, DEL to deselect, F1 for help, Esc to end

Figure 5-3. A cc:Mail user directory, invoked by the "Address to person" command

The directory listing contains the names of the users' mailboxes, the name of a cc:Mail post office that exchanges mail with your local post office, each user's directory status and title, and the date and time a user or post office last exchanged messages with your post office.

The directory may also contain the name of a remote post office. In this case, you must personally know the name of the user on that post office. When you select the post office, you are asked to type in the name. cc:Mail will accept any name you type and send the message for delivery. If you fail to enter the name correctly, however, your message will be rejected at the other end.

Note: Do not worry about how cc:Mail delivers the messages, particularly if you see the names of people who are on non-cc:Mail systems. cc:Mail's directory has routing information for every user, including those who are on fax machines. You can send a message transparently regardless of who you select. Keep in mind, however, that not all mail systems to which cc:Mail connects can receive formatted or graphics files. In general, if you are sending to a non-cc:Mail user, it is best to send text only unless you know for certain that the user can handle a formatted or graphics file.

The directory tells you the status of users as follows:

- L (Local) is a local user on the cc:Mail post office.

- R (Remote) is a user who exchanges mail with the post office from a personal computer via modem.

- r (remote) is a person who exchanges mail with your post office via another cc:Mail post office.

- P (Post Office) is a post office that exchanges mail directly with your post office.

- p (post office) is a post office that exchanges mail with your post office via another post office.

- a (alias) is an alias for a user listed elsewhere in the directory. Quite often, a secretary or department head assumes an alias so that messages can be sent to a job title or department, rather than to an individual's name.

Messages to individuals are sent to their mailboxes as soon as the overall network delivers its messages. Local messages are delivered immediately from you to the mailbox of the recipient. If the recipient has the cc:Mail Notify or Messenger program running, he or she will be notified automatically. Remote messages destined for another post office are delivered on a predetermined schedule, such as hourly or daily, as set by your cc:Mail administrator. Most systems communicate once or twice a day on a regular basis. Messages sent to remote users are not delivered until the remote user dials in to pick up his or her messages.

To select an address, move the cursor to a name and press **ENTER**. Use the **PgUp** and **PgDn** keys to scroll pages of names. If you type the first few letters of the recipient's name, cc:Mail will jump you to that point in the alphabet, so you can begin scrolling closer to the recipient's name. This feature is particularly helpful in large directories.

When you select a name, you remain in the directory to select other names. If you have selected a name you now want to delete, move the cursor to that user's name and press the **Del** key (this command is new with Version 3.15). When you have selected everyone you want, press **Esc** to return to the Address Menu.

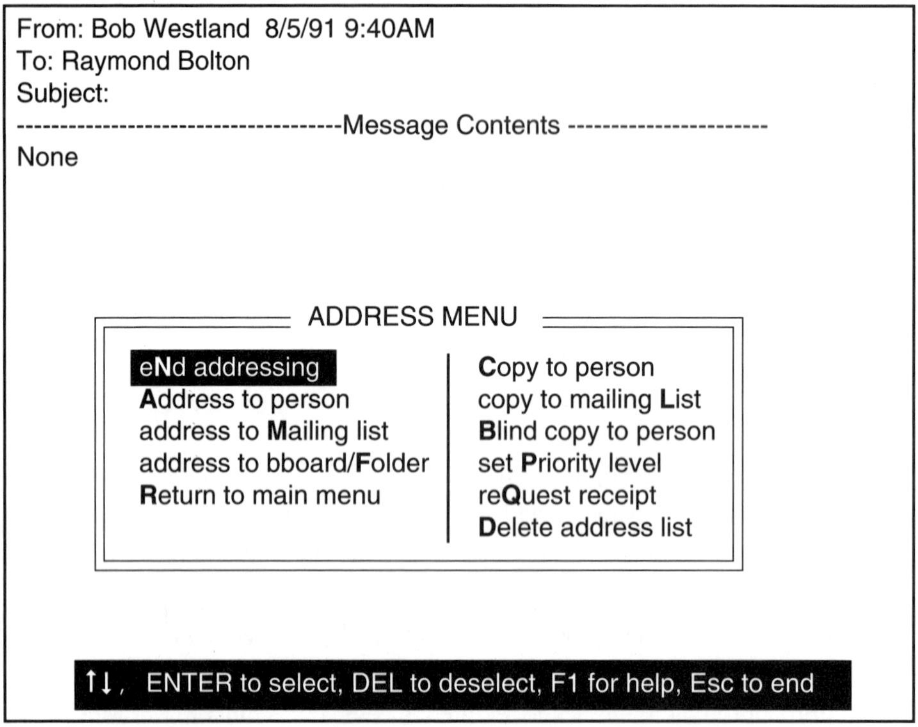

```
From: Bob Westland  8/5/91 9:40AM
To: Raymond Bolton
Subject:
--------------------------------------Message Contents ----------------------
None




                          ADDRESS MENU
        ┌──────────────────────────┬──────────────────────────┐
        │  eNd addressing          │  Copy to person          │
        │  Address to person       │  copy to mailing List    │
        │  address to Mailing list │  Blind copy to person    │
        │  address to bboard/Folder│  set Priority level      │
        │  Return to main menu     │  reQuest receipt         │
        │                          │  Delete address list     │
        └──────────────────────────┴──────────────────────────┘


   ↑↓ ,  ENTER to select, DEL to deselect, F1 for help, Esc to end
```

Figure 5-4. The Address Menu with the "Delete address list" command

You can use the command "**D**elete address list" to delete the entire address list if you want to begin again.

When you have finished addressing to people, you can then address to mailing lists or bulletin boards/folders. You can also send copies and blind copies.

Sending Copies and Blind Copies

The heading "cc:" for a "carbon copy" sent to people other than the primary recipient survived the days of carbon paper into the age of photocopiers, and continues to this day in electronic mail.

Many systems allow blind carbon copies. While a cc: is listed on the memo, recipient(s) of bccs do not appear on the message.

To send copies or blind copies, select the appropriate command and then select recipients just as if you were selecting them for the To: field. When you are finished, press **Esc** to return to the Address Menu. Keep in mind that readers will see the names of those selected for copies, but will not see the names of those selected for blind copies. Blind-copy recipients, however, will see the name of all recipients, including the names of all other people in the bcc: field.

Mailing Lists

A mailing list is a group of names combined under a single heading, such as all of the people in the marketing department under the name of Marketing. A message sent to a list is sent to everyone on the list.

cc:Mail has two types of mailing lists—public and private. Public lists are created by the cc:Mail administrator, while private lists are created by the user. To use a list, select the "address to **M**ailing list" command from the Address Menu. A window pops up over the message screen that shows your bulletin boards/folders and mailing lists:

```
┌─ cc:Mail ── Msgs New ── Bulletin Boards/Folders ─── Msgs New ─┐
│   Inbox        11    3  │   #Suggestions           18    0      │
│   ----Mailing Lists---Names---   # For All Eyes    15    0      │
│   ▉ Executive Comm  5 ▉      # New Employees        15    0      │
│   #Finance      3           Finance                10           │
│   #Marketing    4           Outbox                  2           │
└───────────────────────────────────────────────────────────────┘
 From: Bob Westland  8/5/91 9:40AM
 To: Raymond Bolton
 Subject:
 ------------------------------------Message Contents ----------------------
 None

 Address to mailing list:




    ┌──────────────────────────────────────────────────────┐
    │   ↑↓ and ENTER to select, F1 for help, Esc to end    │
    └──────────────────────────────────────────────────────┘
```

Figure 5-5. Addressing a message to a Mailing List

Move the cursor to the list you want added to the To: field and press **ENTER**. You may also type in the name of the list at the prompt on the bottom of the screen.

If you want to create a new list, type in its name and press **ENTER**. cc:Mail recognizes that you have selected a new name and pops up the directory. Select the names as if you were addressing a message. When you have finished, press **Esc**. The new list is saved for future use, and added to the To: field of your message as well.

Addressing Bulletin Boards/Folders

Bulletin boards and folders are very similar in structure, although they function in very different ways. A bulletin board is a specialized folder created by the cc:Mail administrator that can be accessed by all users at the local server. All local users can post messages to, and read from, the bulletin boards. Folders are private, and are created to store messages for a specific individual.

If you know you want to have a message sent to a bulletin board or saved to a folder, you may send the message directly. Select the "address to bboard/Folder" command. A cc:Mail window pops up that includes the Inbox and mailing lists. The cursor is on the Bulletin Boards/Folder window:

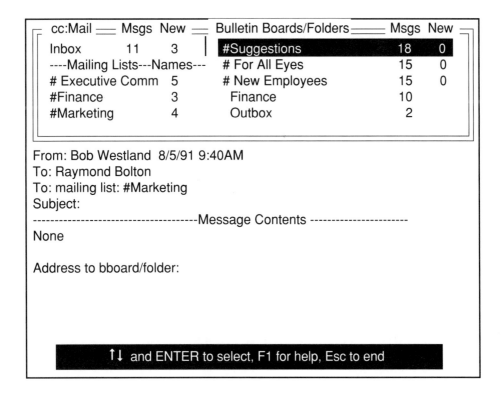

Figure 5-6. Addressing a message to a bboard/folder

Move the cursor to the correct bulletin board or folder and press **ENTER**. When you are finished, press **Esc**. You can create a new folder just as you can create a new mailing list. Type in the name, and the folder is assigned to you.

Note: Some mail systems have an Outbox for messages that have been sent, or are in the process of being created. cc:Mail does not have an Outbox. If you want an Outbox, create a folder called "Outbox" and send your messages there to keep a record of them. You can also create a separate folder or the Outbox folder you have created for messages that are in process but that have not been completed.

Selecting Return Receipt

Within the Address Menu, you can select a return receipt by using the "reQuest return" command. This works just like a postal return receipt: when the recipient selects the message to read, a notice is sent back to the sender.

Note: A return receipt guarantees that a message has been received. It does not guarantee that the message has been read. The same is true for all cc:Mail messages. While the recipient may have entered the Read command, it does not mean that the recipient has read the message.

Setting Priority Level

In cc:Mail Version 3.15, you can set the priority level of a message to Normal, Low, or Urgent. When you select the "set **P**riority level" command in the Address Menu, you are prompted:

Enter priority level (Normal, Low, or Urgent):

Type in **N**, **L**, or **U**. The priority determines the order in which a message will be sent. Frankly, because messages are delivered in seconds on the LAN, and because priority does not impact the time at which mailbags are exchanged, the availability of a message priority within cc:Mail is not very important. In most cases, you can denote priority in the subject field just as easily.

Creating the Message

Entering the Subject

After addressing the envelope with name(s) from the directory, mailing lists, bulletin boards, or folders, select the "e**N**d addressing command." You are placed in the subject field, which is 60 characters in length. Type in the subject and press **ENTER**. You are then placed in the editor to create your first text item. The subject appears in the subject field:

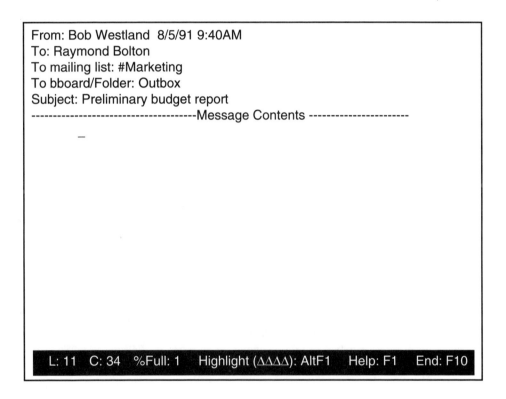

```
From: Bob Westland  8/5/91 9:40AM
To: Raymond Bolton
To mailing list: #Marketing
To bboard/Folder: Outbox
Subject: Preliminary budget report
-------------------------------------Message Contents ----------------------
       _
```
```
    L: 11   C: 34   %Full: 1   Highlight (∆∆∆): AltF1   Help: F1   End: F10
```

Figure 5-7. Entering the editor with the subject field

At this point, you may leave the editor and send the message with just the subject if you want. (The subject field may be long enough for a short answer to a previous message.)

Creating Text Items

cc:Mail has a simple text editor for creating text items of up to 20,000 characters. Except for the ability to create highlighted text blocks, cc:Mail's editor is relatively simple to use. If you are familiar with WordStar and Word Perfect, you'll be able to use the cc:Mail editor with ease, particularly for short messages. For longer messages, you may want to create the file in your own word processing program and attach the file to a short message. You can also save the message as an ASCII file from your word processing program and load the file into the cc:Mail editor.

The full workings of the PC editor are detailed in Appendix A. You can type in text with word wrap and use the cursor keys to move around and delete characters. When you have finished typing your message, press **F10**.

Creating a message in cc:Mail has one major drawback: there is no simple way to save your file. If your PC or LAN crashes while you're creating a message, you will have to start over from scratch. If you plan to create a long message, consider creating it offline in a word processing program in which files can be named and saved. When finished, load it into the cc:Mail editor or simply attach it as a PC DOS file, with a short explanatory message written in the cc:Mail text editor.

If you do use the cc:Mail editor to create your message, you can copy its contents to an ASCII file periodically as a means of saving the message. While this isn't as convenient as a Save command in a word processing program, it will get the job done.

You cannot temporarily store a message you're working on before you send it. The best alternative is to create a folder for messages that you're working on but not ready to send. Send incomplete messages to that folder, so that later they can be retrieved, edited, and sent. Do not attach the recipients' addresses until you are ready to send the completed message.

The Send Menu

When you have finished your text and pressed the **F10** key, the Send Menu pops up:

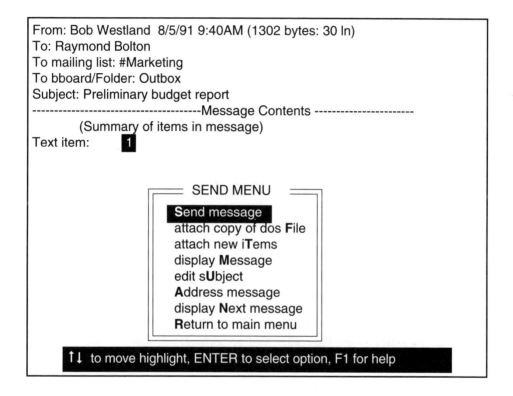

Figure 5-8. Sending a finished text message

Notice that you have a summary of the items in the message, along with a description of the total size of the message on the first line. You can perform any of the commands in the Send Menu. This is the point where you can attach DOS files, graphics, or other items.

Attaching Files to Your Message

Any file on a computer disk can be attached to a cc:Mail message and sent to a recipient. This includes word processing files with formatting, spreadsheets, databases, graphics, sound files, and executable programs.

You can attach up to 20 items to a single message. This means that in addition to communicating with your correspondents, you can show them what you are talking about.

Attachments are received in their original format. This means that if you attach, for example, a Lotus 1-2-3 file to your message, the recipient should be able to read it (provided, of course, the recipient has Lotus 1-2-3).

To attach an item, select "attach copy of dos **F**ile" or "attach new i**T**ems" from the Send Menu.

Attaching DOS Files

If you want your message to have any kind of DOS file attached, select the "attach copy of dos **F**ile" command.

When the command is selected, the Summary Window remains on the screen. Below this appears a command prompt (e.g. "**A**ttach copy of dos file:"), the current file path, and a menu listing the contents of your current directory.

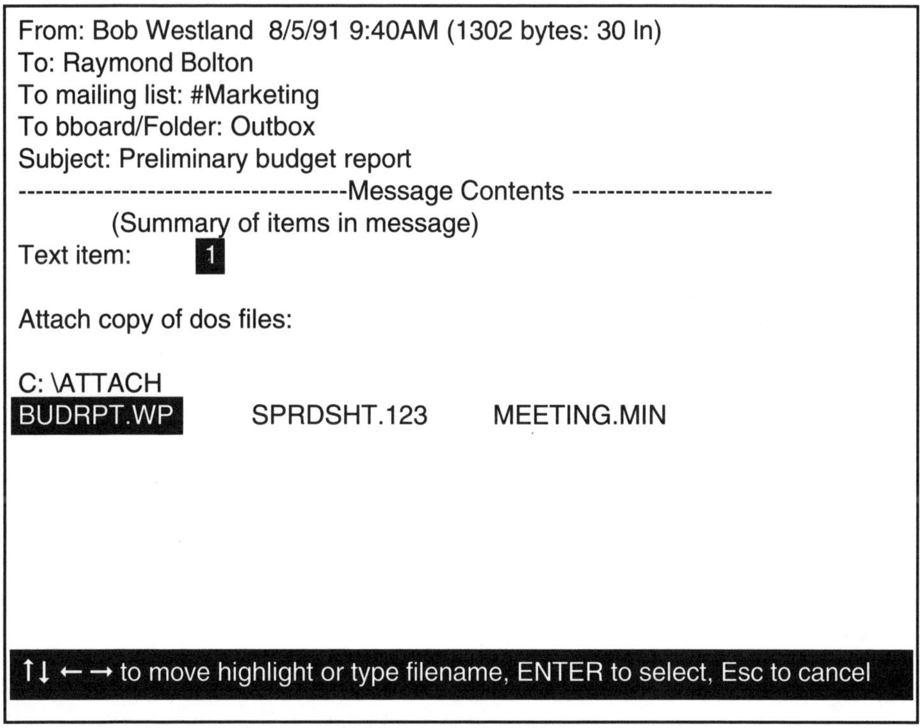

```
┌──────────────────────────────────────────────────────────────┐
│ From: Bob Westland  8/5/91 9:40AM (1302 bytes: 30 ln)         │
│ To: Raymond Bolton                                             │
│ To mailing list: #Marketing                                    │
│ To bboard/Folder: Outbox                                       │
│ Subject: Preliminary budget report                             │
│ ---------------------------------Message Contents ------------ │
│         (Summary of items in message)                          │
│ Text item:      █1█                                            │
│                                                                │
│ Attach copy of dos files:                                      │
│                                                                │
│ C: \ATTACH                                                     │
│ █BUDRPT.WP█        SPRDSHT.123       MEETING.MIN               │
│                                                                │
│                                                                │
│                                                                │
│                                                                │
│                                                                │
│ ▐ ↑↓ ←→ to move highlight or type filename, ENTER to select, Esc to cancel ▌ │
└──────────────────────────────────────────────────────────────┘
```

Figure 5-9. Attaching a DOS file to a message

Move the cursor to the desired file and press **ENTER**. The selected file is then attached to the message as the next item. If you want to change directories, backspace over the selected drive and directory and change it to any you can access. cc:Mail will list up to one screen of the files on that directory. Version 3.16 and later will let you use the cursor to display the rest of the list. On earlier versions, you cannot show undisplayed files, but you can use DOS wildcards to narrow the search.

Wildcards are also useful if you cannot remember the exact spelling of a file's name. Let's say you want to copy the DOS file SELECT.DAT from the F:\MYNAME directory, but are not quite sure of the exact spelling of the file. First, edit the directory path to read F:\MYNAME. At the prompt line, type F:\MYNAME\S*.*, followed by **ENTER**. This will show all files that begin with S.

If you wish to select several files, you may do so by pressing **F5** to mark each file. When you have finished selecting the file(s), press **ENTER**. You will be returned to the Send Menu, and a notation will appear on the screen telling you that item 2 is a File item. The original message is item 1. If you've selected multiple files, the screen will give each one a number, such as:

File item: 2 3 4 5

Note: You are limited to a maximum of 20 items, regardless of file format.

Attaching Other Items

In the example we are creating, the user selects one DOS file. After its selection, the screen appears as follows:

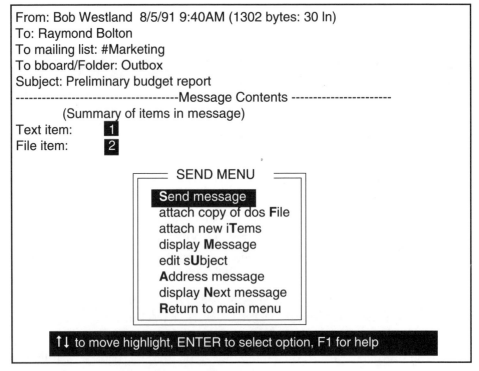

```
From: Bob Westland  8/5/91 9:40AM (1302 bytes: 30 ln)
To: Raymond Bolton
To mailing list: #Marketing
To bboard/Folder: Outbox
Subject: Preliminary budget report
---------------------------------------Message Contents ----------------------
          (Summary of items in message)
Text item:      1
File item:      2

                    ┌──────  SEND MENU  ──────┐
                    │  Send message           │
                    │  attach copy of dos File│
                    │  attach new iTems       │
                    │  display Message        │
                    │  edit sUbject           │
                    │  Address message        │
                    │  display Next message   │
                    │  Return to main menu    │
                    └─────────────────────────┘

     ↑↓ to move highlight, ENTER to select option, F1 for help
```

Figure 5-10. Screen after attaching a DOS file

You are back at the Send Menu, and you can either send the message or continue attaching several kinds of items in addition to DOS files—including text items, graphics items, snapshots, and items from bulletin board/folder messages. The method is similar for each type of item:

- Select the "attach new i**T**ems" command from the Send Menu.

- Select the specific type of item from the Attach Menu that pops up.

- Either prepare the item or select it from the directory where its file resides.

- Enter an item title if it doesn't already have one; i.e., a DOS file name.

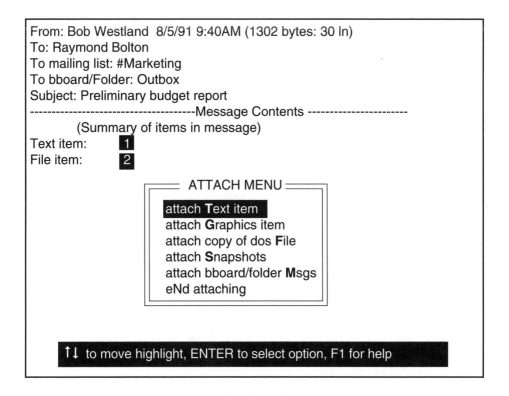

Figure 5-11. The Attach Menu, ready to attach an additional text item

The commands work as follows:

attach **T**ext item

This command puts you in the cc:Mail editor. Create your message and press F10. You are asked to enter a title for the item, which is assigned a new number. See Appendix A for more information on editing text.

attach **G**raphics item

This enters the cc:Mail graphics editor, a drawing program. Create your graphic and press F10. You are asked to enter a title for the item, which is assigned a new cc:Mail item number. See Appendix B for more information on drawing in cc:Mail.

attach copy of dos **F**ile

This provides you with a directory and a menu of DOS files to attach, just as in the earlier section.

attach **S**napshots

This command is similar to the "attach copy of dos **F**ile command," except that cc:Mail labels the items as snapshots in the time listing. You must have taken snapshots of screens with the separate snapshot program provided by cc:Mail before you can use this command (see Appendix C). Text snapshots are saved to a file that you have designated, while graphics snapshots are saved to numbered files, such as SNAP???.001 or SNAP???.002. The SNAP is provided by the program, the ??? depends on the graphics format, and the number designates the order in which the file was saved in that directory. When the "attach Snapshots" command is invoked, type in the name of the directory and select the appropriate snapshot(s). Mark multiple snapshots with the F5 key. When you press **ENTER**, all the snapshots you selected are loaded as appropriate.

attach bboard/folder **M**sgs

This command allows you to attach messages that are stored in cc:Mail to your message. This function is described in the next section.

Attaching Messages and their Items from your Bulletin Board/Folders

The "attach bboard/folder **M**sgs" command lets you attach stored messages from your post office, as well as any or all items attached to those messages.

To use this function, you should know ahead of time the folders and message numbers of the messages you want to attach.

When this command is invoked by selecting "attach bboard/folder **M**sgs" from the Attach Menu, you see a window that lists your bulletin boards and folders. You also are given the prompt: "Attach msgs from bboard/folder:". You can move the cursor to the bulletin board or folder you want and press **ENTER**, or you can type in the name of the bulletin board or folder (or enough of the name to uniquely identify it).

cc:Mail then prompts you to enter the numbers of the messages stored in the bulletin board or folder. Type in the numbers using a comma between non-contiguous numbers and a dash between a range (for example, 1,3,5-8). cc:Mail displays the message and any attachments in sequence, and gives you a chance to reedit the attachment. If you have no changes to make, press **ENTER**. If you have changes and have finished editing the item, press **F10.**

Press **Esc** to stop adding items at any point. If there is an item in the middle of the sequence and you do not want to add it, but you want to add other items later in the sequence, just add it now and delete it later. Pressing **ENTER** after the last item places you back at the Attach Menu. Note that cc:Mail will not warn you if you select a non-existent message number.

It is very easy to become disoriented using the "attach bboard/**F**olders" command if you select multiple messages. cc:Mail will display every item from every message in the sequence. You can either press **ENTER** to accept the item, or you can choose to edit the item, which means you must press **F10.** The **Esc** key ends the sequence. Practice using this command before you select multiple messages.

Displaying and Changing Attachments

After you have finished attaching items, use the "eNd attaching" command to return to the Send Menu, where you will see a "display Message" command. (This command is displayed when there is at least one item in the message.)

If more than one file has been attached in the example we are creating, when the "display Message" command is selected, you are shown the Action Menu. Normally, the Action Menu is not displayed during message creation. During the creation of a multi-item message, the Action Menu shows the following:

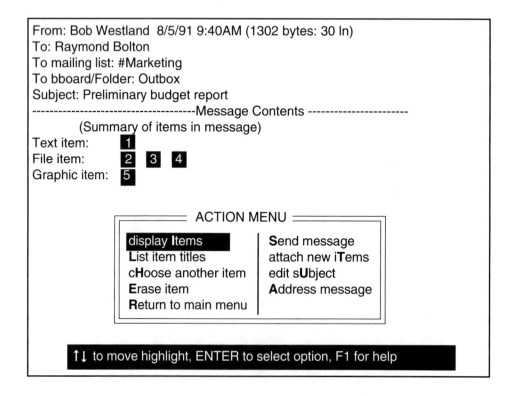

Figure 5-12. Using the Action Menu to display items in a message

Because cc:Mail allows you to attach so many files to a message, it also gives you some tools to organize your attachments. You can list your attachments, give

CREATING AND SENDING MESSAGES

them names, and change their order, so that your recipients will be able to access attachments more easily. The Action Menu lets you use the following commands:

"List item titles" displays a list of items, and "cHoose another item" lets you use the cursor to select a file from the list. The default title is the DOS name of the file, with its creation date and time. Once you are in the item list, you may edit the titles or reorder the list. Use the cursor to move up and down through the listings. You may also press F5 or F6 to mark an item, which highlights the item and displays a small triangular pointer. As you move the cursor to another location in the list, the pointer moves with you and sits between items, so you know exactly where you can move or copy the item. Pressing **ENTER** moves the item if you marked it with **F5,** and copies it if you marked it with **F6**. As you rearrange the items, their numbers change, which determines the order in which they are displayed.

"cHoose another item" lets you use the cursor to select a specific item number, the "display Items" command shows the item, and the "Erase item" command deletes the highlighted item. You can edit a displayed item, unless it is a DOS file or fax item.

Returning to the Main Menu

In virtually every menu, you have the option to "Return to main menu." This command takes you out of the message creation process. A prompt warns you that if the message or changes have not been stored, you will lose the message or any changes you've made.

Sending Messages

When you have finished creating the message and attaching all of the text, graphics, DOS files, and messages stored in your bulletin board/folders, select the "Send message" command. Your message will be sent to the cc:Mail post office for delivery. You can select the "Send message" command from the Send Menu or from the Action Menu.

Sending Fax Messages

cc:Mail's optional program, cc:Fax, interfaces you to the fax network. This program enables you to send a message to any fax machine. The message can only contain information entered using the cc:Mail text editor or graphics editor, or a monochrome .PCX file attached as a "fax item." These items will be sent in sequence as created within a message.

Sending fax messages is transparent to cc:Mail. Fax users are placed in the cc:Mail directory, so that they can be selected as regular cc:Mail users. They will have the designation R, for remote. You can also send a fax to a telephone number not listed in the directory.

CHAPTER 6

Managing Stored Messages

cc:Mail allows you to store messages and retrieve them from bulletin boards or your folders using the "reTrieve messages" command from the Main Menu and then the Retrieve Menu:

Figure 6-1. The Main Menu set to retrieve messages from a bulletin board or folder

Retrieving Messages

Messages can be stored in two places—in your personal folders and in your archives. You can also access messages stored in bulletin boards. The Retrieve Menu commands are shown in Figure 6-2.

```
┌──────────────────────────────────────────────────────────────────────┐
│  ┌ cc:Mail ── Msgs  New ── Bulletin Boards/Folders ── Msgs  New ┐      │
│  │  Inbox        11    3   │   #Suggestions              18    0 │      │
│  └──────────────────────────────────────────────────────────────┘      │
│   There are 71 messages in all.                                         │
│                                                                         │
│                                                                         │
│                                                                         │
│         ┌═════════════════ RETRIEVE MENU ══════════════════┐            │
│         │ ▐retrieve from bboard▌   │  search for New messages │         │
│         │  retrieve from Inbox     │  search by Person        │         │
│         │  scan message Headings   │  search by Keyword phrase │        │
│         │  Act on messages         │  search by Calendar date │         │
│         │  retrieve from archiVe file │ search by priority Level │      │
│         │  Return to main menu     │                          │         │
│         └──────────────────────────────────────────────────┘            │
│                                                                         │
│    ▐ ↑↓ ← → to move highlight, ENTER to select option, F1 for help ▌    │
└──────────────────────────────────────────────────────────────────────┘
```

Figure 6-2. Retrieve Menu and screen

If you do not know what messages you want, select the "scan message **H**eadings" command. cc:Mail will display a list of all message headings in your Inbox, bulletin boards, and folders, as shown in Figure 6-3.

```
Inbox
 11  Ronald Adler        8/5/91   110t      Need for meeting
 10  Carlos Castillo     8/5/91   7146tgf   new product outline
  9  Jerry Littler       8/5/91   600tg     Earnings report
  8  Abigail Fraser      8/5/91   240t      A Question?
  7  Raymond Bolton      8/4/91   8000tgf   Consulting proposal
  6  Jerry Littler       8/4/91   350t      report on meeting w/ Johnson
  5  Ronald Adler        8/4/91   800t      prelim report on meeting
  4  Carlos Castillos    8/3/91   2400tf    wp file for editing
  3  Abigail Fraser      8/3/91   1500t     observations
  2  Raymond Bolton      8/3/91   1200t     questions on consulting work
  1  Raymond Bolton      8/3/91   700t      reply to your query
Bulletin Board: #Suggestions
  1  Carlos Castillo     8/1/91   314t      new form for expenses
  2  Abigail Fraser      7/16/91  503t      handling complaints better
  3  Bob Westland        7/12/91  211t      pizza every month Friday
  4  Raymond Bolton      7/11/91  7505tf    try this new menu program
  5  Jerry Littler       7/9/91   250t      better way to handle shipping

  ↑↓  and ENTER to display message, F5 and F6 to select, Esc to end
```

Figure 6-3. A screen listing all messages in the Inbox, bulletin board, and folders

Scanning your message headings can be time-consuming if you have a lot of messages stored in bulletin boards and folders. Use the **Up** and **Down** arrow keys to scroll through the messages, or the **PgUp** and **PgDn** keys to scan entire screens.

If you do not want to read any of the messages after scanning them, press **Esc**. If you want to read a message, highlight it with the cursor and press **ENTER**. You can also press **F5** to mark individual messages, or use **F5** and **F6** to mark the start and end of a block of messages in a bulletin board or folder.

If you know where you want to find specific messages, use the "retrieve from bboard/**F**older," "retrieve from **I**nbox," or "retrieve from archi**V**e File" commands. If you want to read a message, select it with the cursor and press **ENTER**. You can also press **F5** to select individual messages, or use **F5** and **F6** to select the start and end of a block of messages in a bulletin board or folder.

After you select the message(s) you want, press **ENTER.** cc:Mail retrieves the selected message(s) and displays the Action Menu. You can retrieve messages from multiple sources, and also search for specific parameters. If you select only one message, it will be retrieved immediately and displayed.

Searching Messages

cc:Mail lets you to search all of your messages for some very specific parameters, such as all the messages sent during specific time periods, by specific individuals, or with specific phrases in them. You can search for several other kinds of messages as well, such as message numbers and new messages.

When you use the "search for ..." or "search by ..." commands, you are prompted to specify the parameter. In some cases, you may choose from a menu. For example, when you choose "search by **P**erson," you are shown the mail directory. In other cases, such as "search by **C**alendar date" or "search by **K**eyword phrase," you are asked to enter information.

cc:Mail offers the following search parameters:

- **C**alendar date—enter a range using the format of mm/dd/yy.

- **K**eyword phrase—search your subject field and item titles by complete or partial keyword phrases, not by the actual text within messages. You can type in a phrase of up to 30 characters long. cc:Mail will search for the exact phrase, except for upper and lower case letters, so beware of typos here. Note that only the subject field and item titles are searched, not the message items.

- **P**erson—select from the mail directory all of the mail sent to or from a specific person. This is especially valuable if you have had a running e-mail conversation with someone and want to reassemble all of the messages in sequence.

- message n**U**mbers—specify a number, or a group of numbers using the format 1,3,5-8,12. (You can specify numbers in only one folder at a time.)

- priority **Level**—find messages of a particular priority level: Urgent, Normal, or **Low**.

- **New** messages—search for unread messages in your Inbox, bulletin boards, and folders.

Reading and Acting on Messages

Once you have searched your messages and retrieved them according to your parameters, you may find one message or dozens.

Single Messages

If you have one message, cc:Mail displays the message. Press **ENTER** to see the 4 for more information on what your options are here.)

Multiple Messages

Let's say you have searched and found six messages. Select the "Act on messages" command and the following Action Menu is displayed:

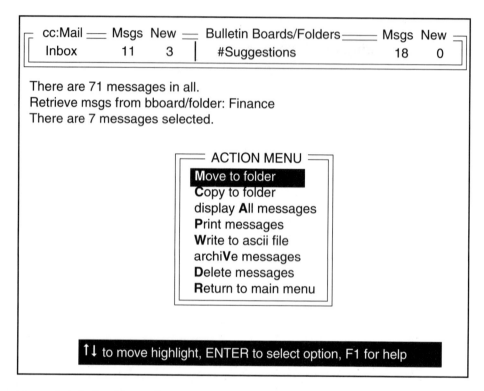

```
┌ cc:Mail ── Msgs New ── Bulletin Boards/Folders ── Msgs New ┐
│   Inbox        11    3  │    #Suggestions          18    0  │
└─────────────────────────────────────────────────────────────┘

There are 71 messages in all.
Retrieve msgs from bboard/folder: Finance
There are 7 messages selected.

                    ┌═══ ACTION MENU ═══┐
                    │ Move to folder    │
                    │ Copy to folder    │
                    │ display All messages │
                    │ Print messages    │
                    │ Write to ascii file │
                    │ archiVe messages  │
                    │ Delete messages   │
                    │ Return to main menu │
                    └───────────────────┘

  ┌──────────────────────────────────────────────┐
  │ ↑↓ to move highlight, ENTER to select option, F1 for help │
  └──────────────────────────────────────────────┘
```

Figure 6-4. Action Menu after selecting the "Act on Messages" command

These commands treat the entire group of messages you have selected as if they were a single message. Here are the basic commands:

- "Move to folder" places all messages in a folder. Select the folder from a list. Press **ENTER** to move the messages to the selected folder. (Keep in mind that this action will remove the messages from their current folders.) You can create new folders by entering a new folder name.

- "Copy to folder" places a copy of the messages in a selected folder and leaves the originals in their current folder. cc:Mail does not duplicate the actual messages; it keeps only one copy. It just creates new pointers to the original. You can create new folders by entering a new folder name.

- "display **A**ll messages" takes you through each item in each message selected in sequence. You can act on each message as if reading it separately.

- "**P**rint messages" prints all the messages in sequence.

- "**W**rite to ascii file" lets you save the messages as one text file in an ASCII file, or allows you to redirect to a printer other than your default printer. You choose the name. If you select COM1, 2, 3, 4, or an LPT that is not the one cc:Mail is told to print to, you can redirect the messages there on a one-time basis. Text and graphics items that are attached to the message will appear in the ASCII file. If the message has DOS file attachments, their names (but not their contents) will appear in the ASCII file. Be careful to choose a new name for your new file. If you choose the name of an existing file, it will be overwritten by your new file.

- "archi**V**e messages" lets you transfer from the cc:Mail server to your own hard disk, or to the network. Archiving to your hard drive, however, saves space on the network server.

- "**D**elete messages" eliminates the messages in one power move. This is a good way to clear out your folders. If you have selected bulletin board messages, it will delete only those you originated. Messages sent to you will be deleted only from your folders and Inbox, not from the system.

In most cases, the commands are executed in a single step (such as deleting messages). In the case of the "display **A**ll messages" command, you are shown every item from every message in sequence. Be careful: it is easy to get lost inside a stack of messages. You can end the review at any time by pressing **Esc**.

USING CC: MAIL

CHAPTER 7

Managing Your Mailbox

The "**M**anage mailbox" command on the Main Menu lets you view the mail directory, manage personal mailing lists and folders, change your password, and select printer types and ports.

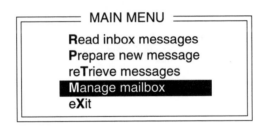

Figure 7-1.The cc:Mail Main Menu's Manage Mailbox command

These are the Manage Menu commands:

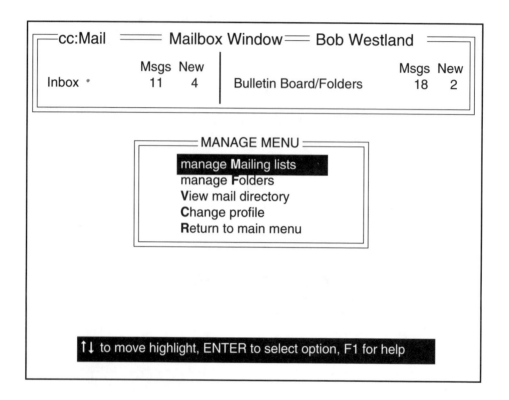

Figure 7-2. The Manage Menu commands

Managing Mailing Lists

When you select the "manage Mailing lists" command, a screen pops up with your Inbox, mailing lists, and bulletin boards. Each mailing list is named, and includes the total number of names in the list. There are two types of lists: private lists that you create, and public lists created by the administrator. Public lists are designated with the pound sign # and cannot be altered. A prompt at the top of the screen says, "Add new title or select existing mailing list:".

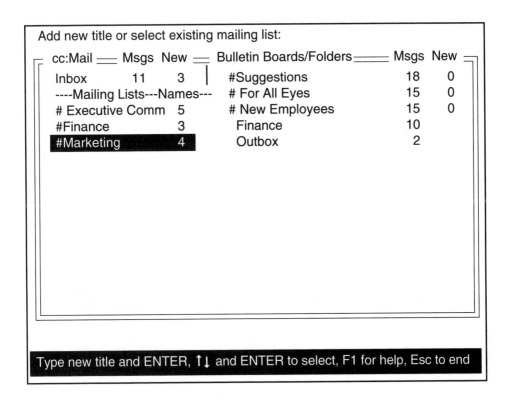

Figure 7-3. The managing mailing list screen

If you type in a new mailing list name, you are placed in the mail directory to select names for the new list.

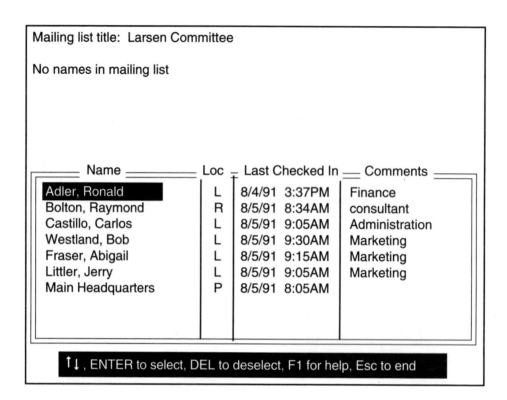

Mailing list title: Larsen Committee

No names in mailing list

Name	Loc	Last Checked In	Comments
Adler, Ronald	L	8/4/91 3:37PM	Finance
Bolton, Raymond	R	8/5/91 8:34AM	consultant
Castillo, Carlos	L	8/5/91 9:05AM	Administration
Westland, Bob	L	8/5/91 9:30AM	Marketing
Fraser, Abigail	L	8/5/91 9:15AM	Marketing
Littler, Jerry	L	8/5/91 9:05AM	Marketing
Main Headquarters	P	8/5/91 8:05AM	

↑↓ , ENTER to select, DEL to deselect, F1 for help, Esc to end

Figure 7-4. A Mail directory, from which names are selected to create a mailing list

To create a mailing list, move the cursor down to the name you want, or type the first few letters of a name and press **ENTER**. Continue selecting names until the list is complete and then press **Esc**.

If you select a public mailing list, you are only allowed to view it. If you select an existing private list, you see the Mailing List Menu:

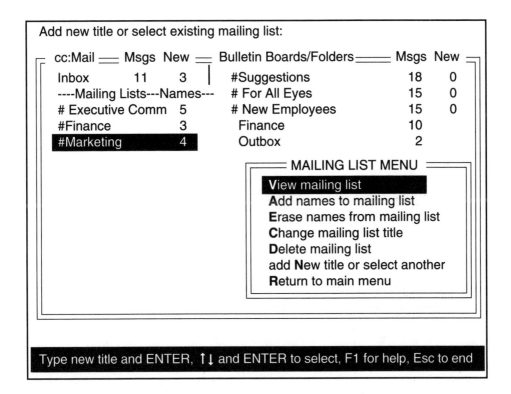

Figure 7-5. The Mailing List Menu

You can move the cursor to any of the above commands to perform actions on the list you have selected. Possible actions include:

- View mailing list—lets you look at the names in the list (which pops up in a separate screen).

- Add names to mailing list—pops up the mail directory so you can add new names to the list just as if you were creating a new list.

- **E**rase names from mailing list—pops up a screen with the mailing list and lets you delete specific names. The names are not deleted from the mail directory.

- Change mailing list title—pops up the title of the list and prompts you to change it. You can type in a new title of up to 30 characters.

- **D**elete mailing list—erases the entire list. You are prompted "Are you sure you want to delete the mailing list?" A **Y** for **Yes** deletes the list, while an **N** or **Esc** keeps the list.

- add **N**ew title or select another—lets you create a new list or select another list.

- **R**eturn to main menu—exits the Mailing List Menu and jumps you to the Main Menu.

Managing Folders

cc:Mail tracks folders and bulletin boards together. Bulletin boards are basically public folders created by your cc:Mail administrator that anyone can access, while folders are private and created by individuals to meet their own storage needs. Bulletin boards are listed first and are designated with the pound sign (#).

When you invoke the "manage **F**olders" command from the Manage Menu, a screen pops up showing your bulletin boards and folders. It is the same screen that displays your mailing lists, telling you how many messages are in each bulletin board or folder, and how many of them are new (unopened). Just as with the mailing list, you are prompted to add a new title or select an existing folder.

If you type in the name of a new folder and press **ENTER**, the prompt appears again. If you move the cursor down to the name on a list and press **ENTER**, the Folder Menu pops up:

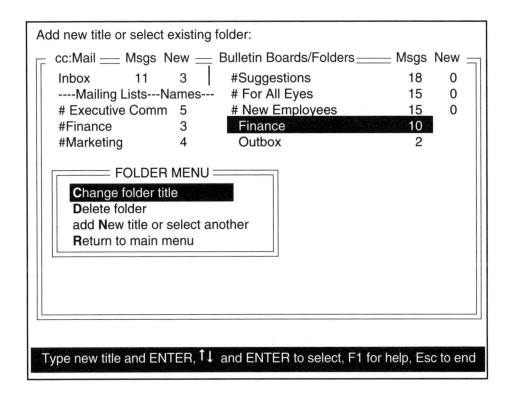

Add new title or select existing folder:

cc:Mail	Msgs	New	Bulletin Boards/Folders	Msgs	New
Inbox	11	3	#Suggestions	18	0
----Mailing Lists---Names---			# For All Eyes	15	0
# Executive Comm	5		# New Employees	15	0
#Finance	3		Finance	10	
#Marketing	4		Outbox	2	

FOLDER MENU

Change folder title
Delete folder
add **N**ew title or select another
Return to main menu

Type new title and ENTER, ↑↓ and ENTER to select, F1 for help, Esc to end

Figure 7-6. The Folder Menu

Move the cursor down to a specific command and press **ENTER** to invoke it. The actions are as follows:

- **C**hange folder title—you are prompted to change the title of an existing folder.

- **D**elete folder—you see the prompt "Are you sure you want to delete the folder?" A **Y** deletes the folder, an **N** or **Esc** keeps the folder intact. Note that when you delete a folder, you also delete all the messages in the folder.

- add **N**ew title or select another—lets you add a new folder or select another one.

- **R**eturn to main menu—jumps you directly to the Main Menu.

Viewing the Mail Directory

When you select the "View mail directory" command, the directory pops up. Unless you are signed on as the cc:Mail administrator, all you can do is look through the listings using the **Up** and **Down** arrow keys to move a line, the **PgUp** and **PgDn** keys to jump a half screen, or the **Ctrl-PgUp** and **Ctrl-PgDn** keys to jump a full screen. You can also type in the first letter of a name, which jumps you to the first entry with that letter—this is particularly valuable for long files. When you are finished, press **Esc**.

Changing Your Profile

When you select the "Change profile" command from the Manage Menu, you are shown the Profile Menu:

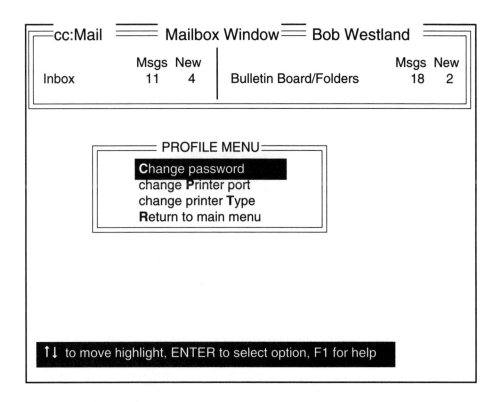

Figure 7-7. Changing your profile using the Profile Menu

When you select the "Change password" command, you are prompted:

Enter old password:

The password is not displayed when you type it in. When you have correctly typed your old password, you will be prompted:

Enter new mail password:

The new password is displayed for you to see as you type it in. Make sure that you remember it exactly as typed. If you forget your password or make a mistake, you must ask your cc:Mail administrator to change the password for you. The password is not case-sensitive; you can type in either upper- or lower-case letters.

At this point you can also select two parameters associated with your printer: the port and the type. When you want to select the port, you are given a list that lets you choose LPT1, LPT2, or LPT3. Move the cursor to the port and press **ENTER**. When you want to select the type, you are given a list that says:

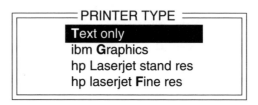

Figure 7-8. Printer type selections

The default mode is text only, but you can use a graphics printer that supports the IBM graphics mode, or an HP LaserJet set up for standard or fine resolutions. If your LAN has both graphics and non-graphics printers, you may change these settings as desired before printing. This is particularly important if you have a printer designated to handle incoming fax messages, such as an HP LaserJet in fine res mode. If you have questions about your network printers, contact your cc:Mail administrator.

CHAPTER 8

The Notify and Messenger Programs

Two special programs supplement cc:Mail's MAIL.EXE program. The first, NOTIFY.COM, tells you if you have new messages available. The second, MESSENGR.EXE, not only notifies you that you have new messages, but also lets you read the messages, send replies, and prepare new messages.

Both are TSR (Terminate-and-Stay-Resident) programs that will operate with any other application program as long as enough memory is available. NOTIFY.COM is 16 kilobytes in size, or 30 bytes when using the HEADINGS or EXTENDED options, while MESSENGR.EXE is 72 bytes. You only need to use one of these special programs—preferably the more powerful MESSENGR.EXE. If you use these programs in conjunction with SNAPSHOT.COM (20K), along with your network, you are using a sizeable amount of memory. Thus, don't plan to use these programs unless you have a PC with at least 1 megabyte, and a DOS memory allocation program that loads and manages TSR programs above the 640 bytes reserved for main applications. If you are unfamiliar with such programs, consult with your cc:Mail administrator.

NOTIFY.COM

The Notify program performs one function: it tells you that you have new messages. cc:Mail does not notify users that they have new messages unless they log in to cc:Mail. Notify, however, automatically loads onto cc:Mail in the background at specified intervals and checks to see if new mail has been placed in your Inbox. The program then pops up a window and makes a beeping noise to let you know that a new message (or messages) is available. If you plan to use Notify, load it into your

PC after logging into the network.

When loaded initially, Notify remains on your screen for five seconds and checks for messages every five minutes. You can specify the time Notify remains on your screen, and the intervals between checks. If you set Notify to remain on your screen until you hit the **Esc** key, you'll never miss a new message. Load NOTIFY.COM using the following command sequence. (This command sequence assumes that the program is stored on the F: drive.)

C> F: NOTIFY [user name] [password] [database location] [option]

Here is an example:

F:NOTIFY JANE WILLIAMS CWPYURL M: CLEAR/0

JANE WILLIAMS is the user name, CWPYURL is the password, the cc:Mail database is on drive M:, the screen will not clear until you hit the **Esc** key. If you neglect to specify the name or password in the above sequence, cc:Mail will prompt you to enter these commands.

If you are on a network that requires a NET USE command to access cc:Mail (your cc:Mail administrator will let you know if you are), enter the Net Use argument after designating the drive where the database files reside. Here is an example:

F: NOTIFY JANE WILLIAMS M:\SRV03\CCMAIL\CCDATA\MARKETING

In this case, SRV03 designates the name of the server, CCMAIL the directory, CCDATA the subdirectory, and MARKETING the network password if required.

Additional parameters that you can specify with Notify should be given at the end of the command line, such as:

C> F:NOTIFY JONES M:\CCDATA CLEAR/0 TIMER/10

Additional parameters include:

- MONO—tells cc:Mail you are using a monochrome monitor with a color graphics card.

- CHKONLY—tells cc:Mail to check once for mail and to then remove the program.

- HEADINGS—displays the headings of new messages. It should only be used if you specify your password. Otherwise, you'll be prompted for your password every time you are notified of new messages.

- EXTENDED—allows you to specify that up to 16 people may use Notify on one PC without the EXTENDED parameter.

- REMOVE—lets you remove the program without having to reboot your PC. This is a valuable command because most people will include NOTIFY.COM in their AUTOEXEC.BAT file, which is used to boot the PC. Instead of having to change AUTOEXE.BAT to take down Notify, you can use the REMOVE option from the regular C> prompt.

- TONE—changes the notification to a tone, rather than a pop-up window. The default is both TONE and WINDOW.

- WINDOW—changes the notification to a pop-up window, rather than a tone.

- ALTx—changes the new-message hot key, which displays the number of new messages you've received since the last check. The default is ALT2.

- CLEAR/<SECONDS>—defines how long the window will stay up on the screen. The default is five seconds. If you specify 0, the window stays up until you press **Esc**. The maximum time allowed is 3,600 seconds.

- TIMER<MINUTES>—specifies the intervals when the cc:Mail database looks for new messages. The default is five minutes. The range is from 1 to 1,440 minutes. If you specify 0, there will be no new-message notification, but the new-message hot key will still be active.

Using Notify

Once Notify is set up, you don't have to do anything to use it; the program simply notifies you if you have messages. When Notify is first loaded, it gives you the number of new Inbox and Bulletin Board messages since it has logged on to cc:Mail. If you choose the HEADINGS option, Notify will display the headings for your Inbox as well. Here is an example:

```
cc:Mail NOTIFY installed for Bob Westland. New message key is Alt-2.
1 new Inbox message
2 new Bulletin Board messages

Carlos Castillo     8/5/91      200t    Thursday meeting
```

Figure 8-1. The Initial Notify Sequence

If you want to log in to cc:Mail because you have new messages, you can use a DOS command to do so automatically. A conditional function in DOS detects that you have new messages and logs you in if you do. If you do not have new messages, the AUTOEXEC.BAT sequence will continue. To use this mode, type IF ERRORLEVEL 1 (cc:Mail log-in sequence). Let's say your normal command line for cc:Mail is F:MAIL WILSON, JANE M:\CCDATA. Here is how the entire command would look in the AUTOEXEC.BAT file:

F:NOTIFY JANE WILSON CWPX M:\CCDATA

IF ERRORLEVEL 1 F:MAIL JANE WILSON M:\CCDATA

If you receive new messages as the day progresses, the cc:Mail window pop ups and your computer beeps to notify you. cc:Mail uses a distinctive doorbell sound for the beep, instead of the typical beep you hear in other programs. If your CLEAR is set to 0, you will be prompted to press **Esc**. If not, the window will disappear by itself in the specified period of time. Notify's message windows, depending upon whether you have the regular Notify or the Notify with headings, look like this:

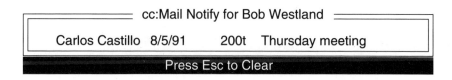

Figure 8-2. Notify message windows

New-Message Key

At any time, you can use the new-message hot key to check to see if you have new messages. The key is set up as Alt-2, but you can change this by specifying a new key when Notify is first run.

Some Anomalies Using High-Resolution Graphics

When you are in some high-resolution graphics modes, particularly if you are not using standard resolutions such as EGA or VGA, cc:Mail's message window will not be displayed, nor will the new message key work. Your PC, however, will still beep, using cc:Mail's distinctive doorbell sound.

Serving Multiple Users

In some situations—for instance, in workgroup situations or when a PC is shared by a number of people—you may want to check the availability of new mail for multiple people on one PC. Up to 16 Notify programs can run in one PC. The only requirement is that each user must have a separate new-message key. If you want everyone's heading listed, use the HEADINGS option. If you do not want to see the headings, use the EXTENDED option. A sample command line is:

NOTIFY Jane Wilson M: EXTENDED ALT2

NOTIFY Pat Paulson M: EXTENDED ALT3

Remember: When the Notify command lines are created, the Alt-x option must be run with a separate Alt key for each user. Each user must either have the HEADINGS or EXTENDED option as well.

The MESSENGR.EXE Program

MESSENGR.EXE has the same notification feature as the Notify program described above, but also allows you to read new messages, make replies, and prepare messages. It is more powerful than Notify and, as a result, is the program of choice unless you have memory restraints.

You load MESSENGR.EXE using the identical sequences as the NOTIFY.COM program, except that you use the command MESSENGR instead of NOTIFY. Two options available with Notify are not required with Messenger: CHKONLY and HEADINGS.

Refer to the Notify section for log-in sequences.

Security Password Feature

Subtle password issues arise for those who choose to use Messenger. Messenger must communicate with cc:Mail once when the program is run in order to load it. For the purpose of this initial communication, you will typically place your password in the command line. Subsequently, when you use the hot key to pop up Messenger over an application program, you are already logged in to cc:Mail. If you want to make certain that nobody can access your cc:Mail files while you step away from your desk and do not mind entering a password every time you use Messenger, you may enter the word PASSWORD after your name when you first log in. This tells cc:Mail to make you enter your password every time Messenger pops up. Here is an example:

F:MESSENGR JANE WILSON PASSWORD M:\CCDATA

Using Messenger

Messenger has the same notification feature as Notify. Once notified, you do not have to leave the program you are working in and then load the MAIL.EXE program. Instead, you press the hot key (default is **Alt-2**), and Messenger pops up. You have two choices:

Figure 8-3. The cc:Mail MESSENGER Menu

Reading Messages

When you invoke the "**R**ead inbox message" command, you see your Inbox summary:

```
╔════════════ cc:Mail Messenger for Bob Westland ════════════╗
║                                                            ║
║  12  Carlos Castillo    8/5/91   200t     Thursday meeting ║
║  11  Ronald Adler       8/5/91   110t     Need for meeting ║
║  10  Carlos Castillo    8/5/91   7146tgf  new product outline
║   9  Jerry Littler      8/5/91   600tg    Earnings report  ║
║   8  Abigail Fraser     8/5/91   240t     A Question?      ║
║   7  Raymond Bolton     8/4/91   8000tgf  Consulting proposal
║   6  Jerry Littler      8/4/91   350t     report on meeting w/ Johnson
║   5  Ronald Adler       8/4/91   800t     last week's meeting
║   4  Carlos Castillos   8/3/91   2400tf   wp file for editing
║   3  Abigail Fraser     8/3/91   1500t    observations     ║
║   2  Raymond Bolton     8/3/91   1200t    questions on consulting work
║   1  Raymond Bolton     8/3/91   700t     reply to your query
║                                                            ║
╚════════════════════════════════════════════════════════════╝
     ↑↓   and ENTER to display message, Esc to end
```

Figure 8-4. Messenger Inbox Summary

You do not see bulletin boards or folders. As in the regular cc:Mail program, all Inbox messages are displayed, with new messages highlighted. Move the cursor to the message you want to read and press **ENTER** to display the message. When you are finished reading the message, press **ENTER** to activate the Action menu (use **F10** if you have used **HOME** or the arrow keys while reading your mail):

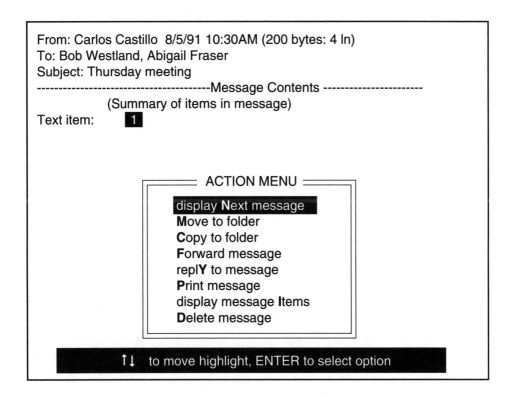

Figure 8-5. The Messenger Action Menu

At this point, you can perform all of the essential tasks associated with reading messages. (See Chapter 4 for more details on how cc:Mail handles reading, but remember that Messenger is a subset of reading in the main MAIL.EXE program, so only essential commands are available.)

Each mail command can be performed in sequence; i.e., you can **F**orward and **P**rint and make a repl**Y,** and either **D**elete the message from the Inbox or **M**ove the message to a folder. You can use any sequence you want. After each command is finished, you will be returned to the Action Menu. Each command works as follows:

- display **N**ext message—takes you to your Inbox to read other messages. When you are finished, press **Esc** to leave Messenger.

- **M**ove to folder—prompts you for the name of a folder to move the message to. You must type the name of an existing folder since you cannot create folders from within Messenger.

- **F**orward message—displays the directory from which you can choose the name of the recipient.

- repl**Y** to message—allows you to prepare a single text item of up to 20 lines with DOS file attachments.

- **P**rint message—lets you print the message to LPT1.

- display message **I**tems—lets you look at different message items, with limitations. All text items will be displayed. DOS files may or may not be displayed depending upon appropriateness, although they can all be detached and copied in a DOS file. Graphics items cannot be displayed.

- **D**elete message—deletes the message from cc:Mail. If it is the only copy, then all references are gone. If the message is stored by someone else, the message remains in cc:Mail, but you lose your ability to access it. You may also edit the displayed message and then address it.

Detaching Files

During the Read message cycle, you are placed in the Action Menu after you have read the first text item. If you have been sent a DOS file as an attachment, the Action Menu will have the command "c**O**py item to dos file." When you select this command, you are prompted for the DOS directory and file name. This is where you specify the location to which cc:Mail stores the file. Note that the file will remain with the message until the message is deleted.

Preparing and Sending Messages

When you select the "**P**repare new message" command after invoking Messenger with the assigned hot-key, Messenger creates a message header and places you in the following Address menu:

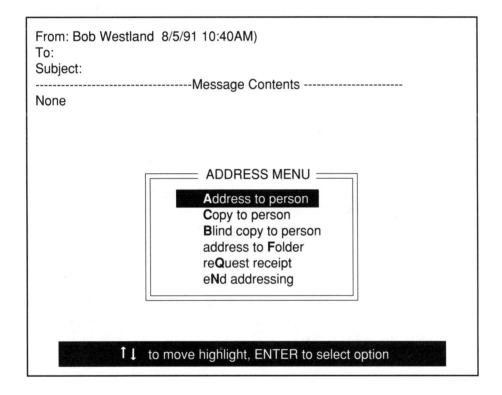

```
From: Bob Westland  8/5/91 10:40AM)
To:
Subject:
------------------------------------Message Contents ----------------------
None




                        ┌──────── ADDRESS MENU ────────┐
                        │                              │
                        │   Address to person          │
                        │   Copy to person             │
                        │   Blind copy to person       │
                        │   address to Folder          │
                        │   reQuest receipt            │
                        │   eNd addressing             │
                        │                              │
                        └──────────────────────────────┘



        ↑↓  to move highlight, ENTER to select option
```

Figure 8-6. The Messenger Address Menu

The "**A**ddress to person," "**C**opy to person," and "**B**lind copy to person" commands all cause the cc:Mail directory to pop up.

```
From: Bob Westland  8/5/91 10:40AM)
To:
Subject:
---------------------------------Message Contents ----------------------
None

Address to person:
 _____ Name _____  Loc _ Last Checked In __ Comments _____
 | Adler, Ronald            |  L  | 8/4/91  3:37PM | Finance         |
 | Bolton, Raymond          |  R  | 8/5/91  8:34AM | consultant      |
 | Castillo, Carlos         |  L  | 8/5/91  9:05AM | Administration  |
 | Westland, Bob            |  L  | 8/5/91  9:30AM | Marketing       |
 | Fraser, Abigail          |  L  | 8/5/91  9:15AM | Marketing       |
 | Littler, Jerry           |  L  | 8/5/91  9:05AM | Marketing       |
 | Main Headquarters        |  P  | 8/5/91  8:05AM |                 |
 |                                                                   |
 |                                                                   |

    ↑↓ ,  ENTER to select, DEL to deselect, F1 for help, Esc to end
```

Figure 8-7. Addressing a message

Move your cursor to the name you want and press **ENTER**. The selected name is added to the To: field. When you are finished selecting addresses, press **Esc**. You are returned to the Address Menu, which has changed slightly so that "e**N**d addressing" is now at the top of the menu, while "**D**elete address list" is at the bottom.

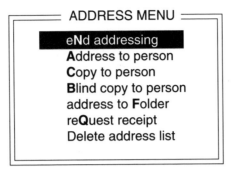

Figure 8-8. Address Menu after entering address

If you want to address the message to a folder, select the "address to **F**older" command. You are prompted:

Address to folder:

In the regular cc:Mail program, you see a list of folders. In the Messenger program, however, you must type in the folder name (you cannot create folders from within Messenger by typing a new name). When you are finished, select the "e**N**d addressing" command. You are placed in the subject field. Enter the subject (up to 60 characters) and press **ENTER**.

You are now placed in the editor where you can enter up to 20 lines of text. The editor is very easy to use, with features such as word wrap (see Appendix A for more information). Messenger has a simplified version of the standard cc:Mail editor that allows only text to be entered. When you are finished typing your message, press

F10. You are placed in the Send Menu.

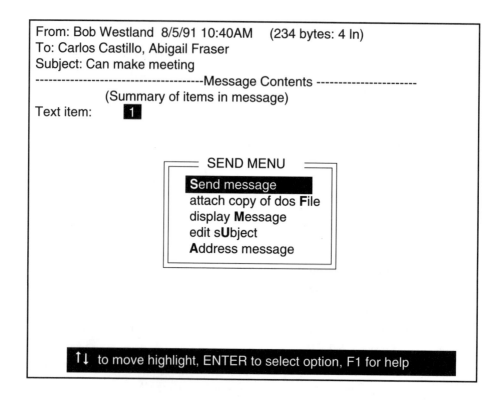

Figure 8-9. The Send Menu in Messenger

At this point, you can attach a DOS file, including a binary file or formatted program file. When you select this command, the current drive and directory is displayed on your local PC, with the files shown on a line underneath. You can backspace over the listed directory and type in another one; that directory's files will quickly be displayed. Move the cursor to the file you want attached and press **ENTER**.

Completing this process places you back in the same Send Menu. You may attach up to 20 total files, add more addresses, or display the message items. When you want to send the message, select the "Send message" command. You are then returned to the Messenger window, where you can press **Esc** to return to your DOS program.

Note: If you do not send the message, you will lose it entirely. If you have started a message and want to edit it further at a later time, send it to yourself or to a folder you have created for messages that are in process. You can then access the message with the regular cc:Mail program for further editing. Keep in mind that the cc:Mail editor does not store messages temporarily on your PC, so if you must reboot your PC or if you lose your network connection while creating a message, it will be lost. Given that you can only store up to 20 lines of text in the Messenger editor, this is of lesser concern than when working in the regular editor that can store 20,000 characters.

The Value of Messenger

Messenger is an excellent program for probably about 90 percent of your mail applications. While there are some complex situations that require the regular mail program, particularly when you must access messages stored in a folder or type in a lot of text, Messenger will meet your needs when you're typing a short message and/or attaching one or two DOS files. Messenger's value, however, must be balanced against its memory requirements (72K RAM).

USING CC: MAIL

CHAPTER 9

Error Messages for PCs

If personal computers were perfect . . . .

We all know they're not. As a result, a critical part of any program is how it handles errors when they occur. Many programs deliver you esoteric messages that have meaning only to the programmer. We've all had experiences where a program has crashed and it says something like, "Error in module DC03:0B16."

cc:Mail tries to give error messages in plain English so that users will understand what the problem is. If you receive an error message while using cc:Mail and you cannot resolve it, contact your cc:Mail administrator. cc:Mail error messages are:

Address buffer full.

You have reached the address limit. To add more addresses to the message, you must send the message more than once. The address limit is approximately 200 names (4 kilobytes).

Block cannot be copied into itself.

When editing a message, you can create text blocks by pressing **F5** at the beginning of the block, and pressing **F6** at the end. You can copy this block of text by moving the cursor to a position outside the block and pressing **Alt-F6**. You cannot press **Alt-F6** and copy the block of text inside itself.

Block cannot be moved into itself.

When editing a message, you can create text blocks by pressing **F5** at the beginning of the block, and pressing **F6** at the end. You can move this block of text by moving the cursor to a position outside the block and pressing **Alt-F5**. You cannot press **Alt-F5** and move the block of text inside itself.

cc:Mail NFT ERROR: Reading post office database

The Network Fault Tolerance (NFT) feature has detected an error in reading your post office database. cc:Mail has been aborted. Press **Esc** to leave the program and clear the error message, then contact your cc:Mail administrator.

cc:Mail NFT ERROR: Writing to post office database

The Network Fault Tolerance (NFT) feature has detected an error in writing to your post office database. cc:Mail has been aborted. Press **Esc** to leave the program and clear the error message, then contact your cc:Mail administrator.

Current directory is write protected.

You do not have sufficient rights to create or write to files in the directory from which you are running cc:Mail, which must be able to create temporary files. Change directories to one in which you have those rights and try running cc:Mail again.

Database drive/directory name too long

The name of the cc:Mail database location exceeds the 23-character limit imposed by DOS. Notify your cc:Mail administrator to change the drive/directory name to a proper length.

Database file already locked.

cc:Mail has tried to lock a database file that is already locked. This is an error that should not occur in normal operations and indicates a potentially serious problem. Contact your cc:Mail administrator.

Database file already unlocked.

cc:Mail has tried to unlock a database file that is already is unlocked. This error should not occur in normal operations and indicates a potentially serious problem. Contact your cc:Mail administrator.

Database file cannot be accessed.

cc:Mail cannot access the cc:Mail database. This means there is some problem with the disk on the server, or with the LAN. It could be as simple as the power being off, if the disk drive is separate from the operating system's drive. It could also indicate a serious problem with the hard drive or database files. Check all hardware, reboot cc:Mail, and try to access the database again.

Database file cannot be found.

cc:Mail cannot find one of its database files on the cc:Mail server. The file may be damaged on the disk, or it may have been deleted.

Database file cannot be locked.

cc:Mail tried to lock a file and has not succeeded. This error should not occur in normal operations and indicates a potentially serious problem. Contact your cc:Mail administrator.

Database file cannot be unlocked.

cc:Mail tried to unlock a file and has not succeeded. This error should not occur in normal operations and indicates a potentially serious problem. Contact your cc:Mail administrator.

Database file not locked.

cc:Mail expected to find a file that was locked, but it was unlocked. This error should not occur in normal operations and indicates a potentially serious problem. Contact your cc:Mail administrator.

Database file too large.

This indicates a possible corruption in the database. This error should not occur in normal operations and indicates a potentially serious problem. Contact your cc:Mail administrator.

Database index out of range.

cc:Mail keeps an index of where each message is stored and lists its parameters within specific ranges. The database has stored a parameter that is out of its defined range. This error should not occur in normal operations and indicates a potentially serious problem. Contact your cc:Mail administrator.

Dates must be entered as mm/dd/yy.

cc:Mail uses the numeric format of month/day/year, such as 12/31/91 (December 31, 1991). Enter the date with the correct format.

Disk error in archiving message.

An error occurred trying to copy your message to an archive file. Try copying the message again to the same archive file and to another archive file. If you cannot do either, it means that the message or both files are damaged, or that you are no longer attached to the network.

Disk error in attaching file.

An error occurred trying to attach a DOS item to a file. The item cannot be attached to a cc:Mail message.

Disk error in copying item.

An error occurred trying to copy a cc:Mail item to a file. Try using another drive and/or directory.

Disk error in reading file.

An error occurred trying to read a file into a text item. The file is damaged and cannot be read into a cc:Mail message.

Disk error in writing message.

An error occurred while the message was being written to an ASCII file. Try the operation using another drive and/or directory to see whether the message is damaged or whether there was a problem writing to the drive/directory.

Error in ALT command line parameter.

cc:Mail allows you to use the **Alt** key with another key, such as **Alt-2** or **Alt-F1**, to perform specific commands. You have used an **Alt**x combination that cannot be used at this point in the program. Study the documentation or ask your cc:Mail administrator to find the correct command.

Error in CLEAR/seconds command-line parameter.

When you are using the Notify or Messenger programs, you can specify how long your screen will display the notification window. You have made an error specifying this parameter and must reenter it.

Error in TIMER/minutes command line parameter.

cc:Mail does not notify you when you have a new message. You can use the Notify or Messenger programs to check for new messages by specifying the interval between checks. You have made an error specifying this parameter and must reenter it.

File cannot be found.

You have specified a file name that does not exist on that drive and directory. Retype the file name.

File does not have archive format.

You have selected an archive file for a message that does not have cc:Mail's archive format. Select a correct archive file or contact your cc:Mail administrator if you believe that you have selected a correct archive file.

File with that name cannot be created.

You have selected a name for a file that does not adhere to DOS conventions. Try another name that falls within the DOS parameter of XXXXXXXX.XXX.

Folder not found.

You have specified a folder name that does not match any folders you have stored in cc:Mail. Try the name again. Contact your cc:Mail administrator if you know you've created a folder and cc:Mail cannot find it.

Help file cannot be found.

The file Mail.hlp is not on the drive and directory in which the cc:Mail post office is located. Contact your cc:Mail administrator.

Help screen cannot be read.

The help file at your cc:Mail post office is damaged. Contact your cc:Mail administrator.

Incompatible database.

cc:Mail separates its database from the LAN program and keeps track of program versions for both. You have a database version that does not work with the LAN program version. To solve the problem, you must upgrade your software properly. Contact your cc:Mail administrator.

Incorrect number of command-line parameters.

When you are starting up cc:Mail, you access the program with a command line that defines who you are and where the program is located. You have not provided enough information in your command line to access cc:Mail correctly. Reenter the command line. Contact your cc:Mail administrator if you have trouble accessing cc:Mail.

Insufficient disk space for database file.

The drive containing the cc:Mail database is full. Notify your administrator that more space must be allocated to the database file.

Insufficient disk space to copy item.

You have run out of disk space at your server. Notify your cc:Mail administrator.

Insufficient disk space to create DOS file.

You have run out of disk space on the drive you specified to create your DOS file. Use a new disk or erase files from the one you specified.

Insufficient disk space to create item.

cc:Mail creates temporary files in your current directory when you attach new items. Your current drive is full. Free up some space and try creating the message again.

Insufficient disk space to store message.

You have run out of disk space at your server and cannot store the message. Notify your cc:Mail administrator. On an interim basis, write your text to a DOS file so it can be reloaded into a message later.

Insufficient disk space to write file.

You have run out of disk space on the disk you have specified. Erase files from the disk or use another one.

Insufficient memory.

You need 320K to run cc:Mail. Either free memory from your PC or add more.

Item cannot be displayed.

You have specified an item that your PC cannot display; for example, you have specified a graphics item and your PC does not have a graphics card.

Item cannot be read.

You have specified an item that is damaged and cannot be read by cc:Mail. Request that the sender check the item and resend a clean copy.

Line number out of range.

cc:Mail allows you to enter a specific range of lines from an ASCII file into the text editor, so that you only load a portion of the file. The line numbers must be positive integers. You have specified line numbers out of range, such as a number larger than the total number in the file. Keep in mind that a line is defined as a RETURN stored in the file.

Line will be too long after replacing.

cc:Mail's editor has a maximum size of 80 characters per line. Setting your margin to 80 characters disables word wrap. Your margin is set to 80 characters and you have requested a search-and-replace operation that will exceed the 80-character limit with word wrap not available. Reformat the line so the operation can be performed.

Mail password not correct.

You have specified a password that is not correct. Try it again. Notify your cc:Mail administrator if there is a problem.

Mail password too long.

You have specified a password that is longer than 10 characters. Try it again with a shorter password.

Maximum number of users exceeded.

A single PC can have the Notify program running for up to 16 separate users. You have reached this limit and must remove a user before adding the next one.

Message buffer full.

You have attempted to retrieve a large number of messages at the same time and the message buffer has filled up. Try retrieving a smaller number of messages.

Message cannot be copied.

A disk error occurred while the message was being copied to a folder at the server. Try the function again. If the problem still exists, contact your cc:Mail administrator.

Message cannot be read.

The message you are trying to access is damaged and cannot be read. Contact your cc:Mail administrator. It may be possible to clear up the problem.

Message cannot be read. Entry deleted.

The message you are trying to access is damaged and cannot be read and will be deleted. If you need the message, contact your cc:Mail administrator immediately to see if the message can be restored from a backup.

Message cannot be sent to username.

You have sent a message to a user that cannot be delivered. Contact your cc:Mail administrator. If a name is in the directory, you should be able to deliver at least the text portion of the message.

Message cannot be stored.

While cc:Mail was trying to store your message on the server, a disk error occurred. Either the temporary storage area housing one of the message items has been damaged, or the area on the hard disk allocated for the message is damaged. If the message can be read on your screen, save it to your hard disk temporarily and contact your cc:Mail administrator.

Message item cannot be copied.

A disk error occurred when trying to copy a message item. The item may be damaged, or the temporary file used cannot be created.

Message numbers must be entered as 1,3,5-8,10 for example.

When using the command line to type in a command associated with messages, you must use commas to delineate single messages and a dash to delineate a range. The numbers you typed could not be interpreted.

Name not found to remove.

You are trying to remove the name of a user from the Notify program, but have not typed the name correctly. Try it again.

Name not in mail directory.

You have entered a name that is not listed in the directory while trying to access cc:Mail. You may have made a typing mistake. Try to re-enter your name. If that does not work, contact your cc:Mail administrator. If an error has occurred, your administrator can get you access to your account again.

New names may not be entered.

You do not have the authority to enter new names in the mail directory. Ask your cc:Mail administrator to enter the name for you.

New titles may not be entered.

You have used up the maximum 200 folders and/or private mailing lists that you can store in cc:Mail, and you cannot create a new one until one or more of the old ones are deleted.

No more characters may be entered.

You have entered more characters than you are allowed. Retry your entry with fewer characters.

Not all files are displayed.

You have asked to see a listing of directory files and there are more in the directory than cc:Mail displays. Enter the specific file you want to see or use a * with some descriptive information to see a subset that will likely display your file.

Page table corrupted.

cc:Mail's internal locking mechanism for writing to the database is corrupted. This error should not occur in normal operations and indicates a potentially serious problem. Contact your cc:Mail administrator.

Page table full.

cc:Mail keeps an internal page table that has become full. This error should not occur in normal operations and indicates a potentially serious problem. Contact your cc:Mail administrator.

Phrase not found.

When editing text, you have asked to find a phrase that is not in the text.

Please type Y for Yes, or ENTER or N for No.

You were asked for a Y, N, or ENTER response and did not provide it. Type in one of the three responses.

Post office cannot be accessed.

When trying to log in to cc:Mail, you have specified that the cc:Mail database files are on a specific drive and directory, but cc:Mail cannot find these files. Please try again with a new drive and directory. Contact your cc:Mail administrator if you cannot get access to cc:Mail.

Printer is unavailable.

You want to print a message or file and your printer is not available. Make sure the printer is connected properly and turned on, and retry the command. If you still have a problem, make sure the printer is set up to print on the same LPTx channel as you specified to cc:Mail. The default is LPT1.

Program cannot be run from a database directory.

You have specified that the cc:Mail program and database be run from the same directory. Convention requires that they be in separate directories. Resubmit your command with the appropriate directories. Contact your cc:Mail administrator if you have a problem.

Remote users may not access mail locally.

You have tried to log on locally, but are defined as a remote user and cannot do so. Have your cc:Mail administrator register you as a local user or dial in via a modem.

Sender name not in mail directory.

The sender who sent you the message and requested a return receipt is not in your mail directory and will not be sent a receipt.

Server name cannot be accessed.

Your PC cannot access the requested server. Make sure you specified the right name, and that the server is available. If everything seems right and you still cannot access the server, contact your cc:Mail administrator. (Then sit calmly in your office and either punch a rubber ducky or let out a loud scream. Even though PCs are supposed to be logical, strange things do happen. The problem will get straightened out, but it will confuse everyone for awhile.)

Server name too long.

Your server can have a name of only up to 30 characters. You have submitted a name longer than 30 characters. Submit a shorter name.

Snapshot cannot be read.

You have requested that cc:Mail create an item that is labeled a snapshot. The file does not appear to be a snapshot. Select the appropriate file or retake the snapshot and retry the command.

Text buffer full.

You have filled your text buffer with 20,000 characters. To continue, you must end the item and start a new one, or copy the item to a file and delete half of it, so you have two items of about 10,000 characters each.

USING CC: MAIL

cc:Mail Remote

USING CC: MAIL

cc:Mail Remote for IBM PCs and Compatibles

This chapter covers cc:Mail Remote version 3.2. cc:Mail was designed as a LAN-based program, but eventually users pinpointed two specific needs not met by the system. First, many needed to access their mailboxes while traveling. Second, users often needed to add a few people to their system from other locations on an ad hoc basis. To meet these needs, cc:Mail created the cc:Mail Remote program, which looks and feels like the cc:Mail LAN program, but can be operated from a stand-alone IBM PC or compatible. cc:Mail Remote is not yet available for the Macintosh.

In the cc:Mail LAN program, you access the cc:Mail server. While the program runs in your PC, all file operations are performed at the server, except for archiving—which can be done optionally on the server as well. All Inbox, folder, and bulletin board messages are stored at the server, along with the directory and mailing lists, public and private.

In cc:Mail Remote, all file operations are performed in your PC, including storing Inbox and folder messages, mailing lists, and a directory of users. The only function you cannot do in cc:Mail Remote is read bulletin board messages; while you can send messages to bulletin boards, you cannot read the responses—unless your cc:Mail administrator has installed the optional "Automatic Directory Exchange." Otherwise, you must have someone forward bulletin board messages directly to you.

The cc:Mail Local-Remote Connection

cc:Mail Remote operates just like the cc:Mail LAN program, except that incoming messages are stored in a local inbox and outgoing messages are stored in an Outbox, until you use cc:Mail Remote to access the remote post office server. When you access the post office, cc:Mail Remote transmits messages from your

Outbox and receives new messages from the post office into the inbox.

cc:Mail Remote's features (the text and graphics editors, the menu structure, the read/reply process, the mail-creation process, and the mailbox maintenance cycle) are just like cc:Mail—except cc:Mail Remote uses a modem and local telephone lines instead of a local area network (LAN), and cc:Mail Remote users must maintain their own user directory.

Note: In most cases, cc:Mail Remote is used to communicate with a central post office. It can be used, however, to connect directly to another remote user; a cc:Mail Remote user dials up another user, who acts as the post office. This is discussed in the section of this chapter on sending and receiving mail.

How cc:Mail Remote Users Can Use This Book

cc:Mail Remote users should read Chapters 3, 4, 5, 6, 7, and 9 on using cc:Mail main functions, along with Appendices A-D on the text and graphics editors, the Snapshot program, and cc:Mail's command structure. (Chapter 8, on using the Notify and Messenger programs, is applicable only to cc:Mail LAN users.)

This section reviews the main differences between cc:Mail and cc:Mail Remote's functions, along with all of cc:Mail Remote's extra features.

The main differences are that cc:Mail Remote has a Store Menu instead of a Send Menu, and the cc:Mail Remote Main Menu has a command to "**S**end/receive messages," while the cc:Mail Main Menu has no such command. The cc:Mail Remote Store Menu is identical to cc:Mail's Send Menu in terms of function and commands. The difference is that the Send Menu sends messages to a post office, while the Store Menu stores messages in your Outbox. Thus, if you are a cc:Mail Remote user, note that the Send Menu corresponds to the Store Menu (discussed in Chapter 5).

cc:Mail Remote's unique functions are associated with:

- Using a modem to dial in to a cc:Mail post office.

- Managing the Outbox.

- Managing a directory of cc:Mail users.

- Managing all of the cc:Mail files on a single PC.

Installing and Running cc:Mail Remote

While cc:Mail is a LAN program in which users are set up by a cc:Mail administrator, cc:Mail Remote does not have an install program. You install it simply by copying its files to the disk and directory you want to run it from. You must choose where to install it. The cc:Mail Remote diskette contains three files:

REMOTE.EXE

REMOTE.HLP

SNAPSHOT.COM

If you want to install the program in a separate directory and do not know how, follow the directions below (if you know how to create directories, create one and copy the files into it).

Installing on a hard disk

1. Go to your root directory by typing **cd ** and pressing **ENTER** at any C> prompt.

2. At the C> prompt, type **mkdir ccmail** and press **ENTER**.

3. At the C> prompt, type **cd ccmail** and press **ENTER**.

4. You will either have a C> prompt or one that reads C (ccmail)>

5. Place the cc:Mail Remote disk in drive A (or B), type **copy a:*.*** and press **ENTER**. The three files will be copied to the new directory.

6. To run cc:Mail Remote, type **remote** and press **ENTER**. Read Appendix C on SNAPSHOT to determine whether you want to run it in your PC.

Installing on a computer with two floppy disks

1. Create two blank, formatted diskettes; label one "Mailbox" and the other "Folder."

2. Put your cc:Mail Remote diskette in drive A and the Mailbox diskette in drive B.

3. Type the command **COPY A:REMOTE.HLP B:**

When you run cc:Mail Remote, put your backup copy of the cc:Mail Remote disk in drive A. Make sure drive A is the current drive with the command

A:

At the A> prompt type the command

REMOTE

After cc:Mail Remote starts up, it will prompt you to insert the Mailbox diskette in drive A, and the Folder diskette in drive B. After you have done this, press **ENTER** to continue.

Installing on a computer with only one floppy disk

When you run cc:Mail Remote, put your backup copy of the cc:Mail Remote disk in drive A. Make drive A the current drive with the command

A:

At the A> prompt type the command

REMOTE A:

Start-up options

When you enter the Remote command, you have 19 optional commands for giving instructions to cc:Mail Remote. These commands are entered at the DOS prompt. For example:

C> remote fifo

C> remote files/c:ccmail\ccdata mono

You can enter multiple commands on one line. If you want to enter a complex sequence that is repeated every time you run cc:Mail, create a batch file that has the commands. Here is an example:

c(ccmail)> copy con mail.bat

remote fifo mono files/c:ccmail\ccdata archive/c:ccmail\ccdata mouse

^Z

Press **F5** to create the ^Z and **ENTER** to complete a batch file. With a batch file entitled mail.bat, you can enter all the commands in that file simply by typing the word **mail**.

The optional commands are:

ARCHIVE/path

This indicates the drive and directory to use for archive operations. The default is the drive and directory where cc:Mail Remote is started.

DR/E, DR/I

This indicates you're using a DataRace external or internal modem.

FIFO

This tells cc:Mail Remote to show the oldest messages in your Inbox first. Normally, you will see the newest messages first.

FILES/path

This sets the path for all cc:Mail Remote operations that access DOS files, such as storing messages for the Outbox and Inbox. Normally, this is the drive and directory where cc:Mail Remote is started.

KEYS/abc

When you run cc:Mail Remote, enter the identified power-user keys, which will invoke certain commands. As an example, you can use this command to instruct cc:Mail to display your Inboxupon logging on instead of remaining in the Main Menu.

LPTx

This specifies the printer port used by cc:Mail Remote. The default is LPT1. Use this command only if you have more than one printer and you want to use a printer other than LPT1.

HSEC/OFF

This command disables error correction in high-speed modems. You will need this only if you are communicating to a server that runs a version of cc:Mail below 3.01.

MODEM/

You will use this to enter special modem commands. (Example: MODEM/ ATM0 will turn off the modem's speaker.) This is normally not required.

MONO

This tells cc:Mail Remote you are using a monochrome monitor with a color graphics card adapter.

MOUSE

This command specifies whether you have a mouse set up for operation. cc:Mail Remote allows you to use a mouse when editing graphics or when invoking Menu commands.

MSGSIZE/size

This command prevents you from sending or receiving a message that is over the specified size in thousands of bytes. A size of 24 is interpreted as 24,000 bytes.

NOR/O

This prevents unexpected receive-only calls from being accepted. Only other users or a post office can dial your workstation, which must be set up to receive incoming calls.

PASSWORD

This command includes your password when you log in to cc:Mail Remote.

PCSLICE

This command is required if cc:Mail Remote is being run on a Convergent Technologies computer.

RECLAIM

This reorganizes the cc:Mail Remote database. Required only if you have a large number of messages stored and want to increase the access speed.

RECLAIM/n

This is used to optimize the update speed if you are adding a large number of users to your directory automatically. The value of n is expressed to the nearest 1,000 names being updated, although you must use the highest value. If updating 2,500 names, for example, n would be 3 for 3,000. The largest value for n is 64.

R/O

This puts cc:Mail Remote in a mode where it will only receive messages; it will not send any messages from your Outbox.

S/O

This command puts cc:Mail Remote in a mode where it will only send messages from your Outbox to the post office; it will not receive any new messages.

TB/E, TB/I

This indicates that you have a Telebit external or internal high-speed modem.

cc:Mail Database Files

cc:Mail Remote creates files you should be familiar with. It must store these files locally, since the server is not available for storage. The files show cc:Mail Remote's basic organization:

- Individual files for each message. The files are named MSGXXXXX, with X representing a five-digit number. The files contain all the text and graphics items, as well as pointers to attached files stored on the PC.

- A file named MBOXDATA contains your Personal and Equipment profile information, along with pointers to messages that are located in your Inbox and Outbox.

- A file named FOLDDATA contains the name of your folders, along with pointers to messages stored in the folders.

- Temporary files labeled SEGXXXXX.XXX hold text and graphics items until the message is stored.

- Two files, FOLDTEMP and MBOXTEMP, are used during the RECLAIM process.

Starting Up cc:Mail Remote

Because cc:Mail Remote is a regular PC program, there is no initial security when you first run the program, unless it has been set up for you in advance by your cc:Mail administrator. Keep in mind that you must be registered at a cc:Mail post office to exchange mailbags. We'll assume that you are already a local user, or that you have been given your name and password. You also need to know the name of the post office and its phone number. If you do not have this information, contact your cc:Mail administrator.

When you first run cc:Mail Remote, the profile window looks like this:

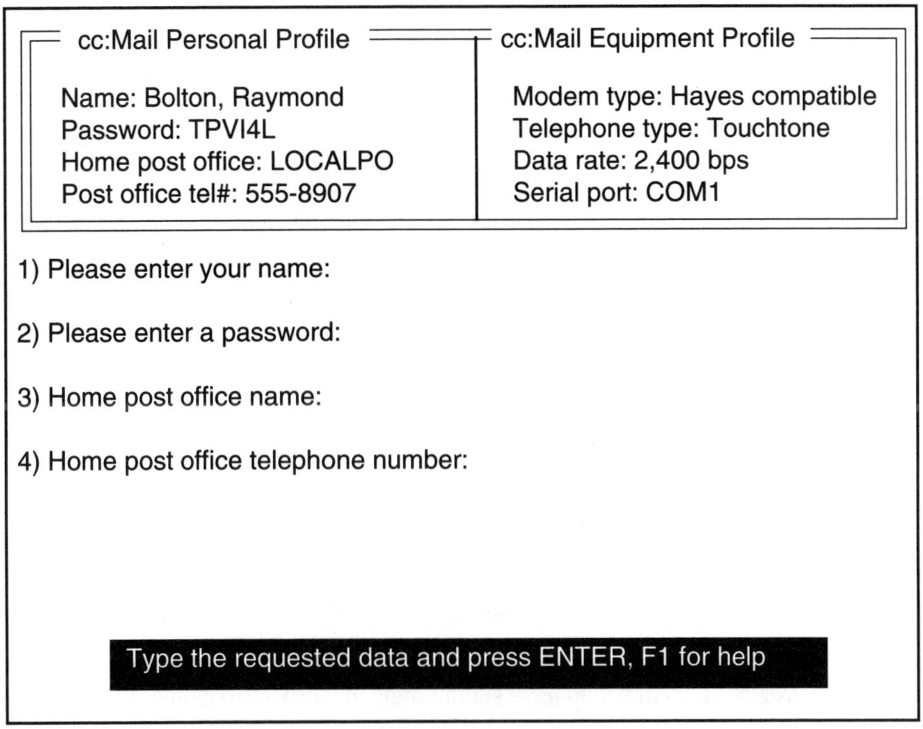

```
┌─────────────────────────────────────────────────────────────────────┐
│  ┌─ cc:Mail Personal Profile ═══════╤═ cc:Mail Equipment Profile ═══┐ │
│  │                                  │                               │ │
│  │  Name: Bolton, Raymond           │  Modem type: Hayes compatible │ │
│  │  Password: TPVI4L                │  Telephone type: Touchtone    │ │
│  │  Home post office: LOCALPO       │  Data rate: 2,400 bps         │ │
│  │  Post office tel#: 555-8907      │  Serial port: COM1            │ │
│  └──────────────────────────────────┴───────────────────────────────┘ │
│                                                                       │
│  1) Please enter your name:                                           │
│                                                                       │
│  2) Please enter a password:                                          │
│                                                                       │
│  3) Home post office name:                                            │
│                                                                       │
│  4) Home post office telephone number:                                │
│                                                                       │
│                                                                       │
│                                                                       │
│         ┌─────────────────────────────────────────────────────┐      │
│         │  Type the requested data and press ENTER, F1 for help │     │
│         └─────────────────────────────────────────────────────┘      │
└─────────────────────────────────────────────────────────────────────┘
```

Figure 10-1. The cc:Mail Remote profile window on login

While there are entries in the Personal and Equipment profile sections, they will be blank when you first log on. cc:Mail Remote walks you through the prompts one at a time; as you fill out the prompts, the entries will be filled out. Your first prompt reads:

Please enter your name:

Your cc:Mail administrator must provide you with your name (which can be up to 30 characters), post office name, and phone number. Enter your last name first followed by a comma. (Example: Bolton, Raymond. cc:Mail interprets this as

Raymond Bolton, but lists the user's last name in alphabetical order.)

The first four prompts allow you to enter your name, password, cc:Mail home post office, and phone number. The password can have up to ten characters or digits. The home post office, also supplied by your cc:Mail administrator, can have up to 20 characters. Your cc:Mail administrator also provides you with the phone number, which can have up to 40 characters (only the first 21 will show). You may also need a script file. If you need to create a script file, your cc:Mail administrator will notify you and give you the script and instructions. This is discussed later in this chapter.

The equipment profile is handled a little differently. You will have the opportunity to set your pen color, margins, modem type, telephone type, data rate, serial port, printer port, and printer type.

The first menu lets you choose your foreground and background colors. The default is white-on-blue, which is usually an excellent choice. If you prefer some other combination, use the **Up** and **Down** cursor keys to choose the background color and the **Left** and **Right** keys to choose the foreground color. The cell in the lower right corner of the menu shows what the result will be. Press **ENTER** after you choose a combination you like, or **Esc** to cancel the process.

Use the **Left** and **Right** cursor keys to set the left and right margins for the cc:Mail Remote text editor. Set the left margin and press **F5**; set the right margin and press **F6**. Press **ENTER** after you have set the margins, or **Esc** to cancel the process.

Next, a window appears in the middle of the screen for you to set your modem type:

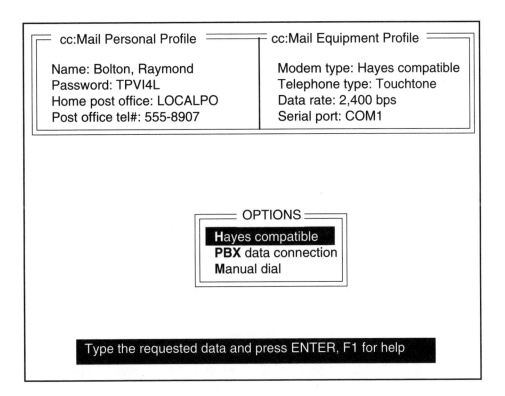

Figure 10-2. cc:Mail Remote Equipment Profile screen.

Move the cursor to your modem type and press **ENTER**. In most cases (unless your cc:Mail administrator has notified you to the contrary) you will have a Hayes-compatible modem.

Next, you are requested to enter telephone type, data rate, and serial port:

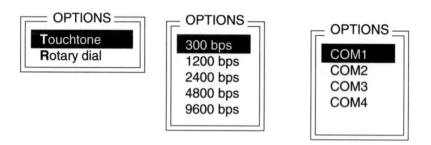

Figure 10-3. Access options

The choices are related to the specifics of your PC. If you are unfamiliar with any of the choices, consult your cc:Mail administrator. Most likely, you will be accessing cc:Mail at 1,200 or 2,400 bps on COM1. Be careful if you plan to use COM3 or COM4. While cc:Mail says the software works fine with these ports, users have reported problems—although they may well be due to users failing to configure the serial port correctly.

cc:Mail Remote Main Menu

After you have set up cc:Mail Remote, the Main Menu appears. Figure 10-4 shows how cc:Mail Remote normally appears when you start the program. In this example, the Main Menu is for a user who was listed as Remote in previous examples.

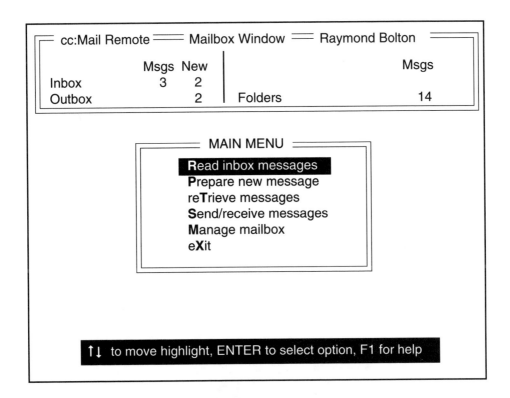

Figure 10-4. The cc:Mail Remote Main Menu

The cc:Mail Remote Main Menu is slightly different than the local cc:Mail Main Menu: there is a "Send/receive messages" command in the Remote version, and there is no option to "**R**ead Inbox messages."

Managing the Mailbox and User Directory

Before you begin to read, create, and send messages, it is important to learn the differences between maintaining the cc:Mail Remote mailbox and the cc:Mail mailbox. In cc:Mail, you can manage mailing lists and folders, change your profile, and view the user directory. In cc:Mail Remote, you must also maintain a directory of users, which is stored on the server. Select the "**M**anage mailbox" command from the Main Menu:

Figure 10-5. The cc:Mail Remote Main Menu at the Manage mailbox command.

You are then placed in the Manage Menu:

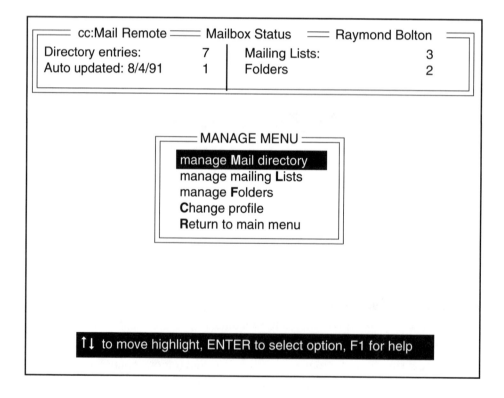

Figure 10-6. The cc:Mail Remote Manage Menu

For more information on managing your mailing lists and folders, refer to Chapter 7. To manage your profile, just repeat the process described earlier for first signing on to cc:Mail.

Manually Managing your Directory

To maintain your directory of users, select the "manage **M**ail directory" command. You are placed in the directory, which consists of a list of names. While it may initially contain only two names, it may eventually contain several thousand.

```
┌──────────────────────────────────────────────────────────────────┐
│ Add new name or select existing name:                            │
│                                                                   │
│      ══ Name ══════════   cc:Mail Address  ═══ Comments ══       │
│   ┌──────────────────────────────┬─────────────────────────┐    │
│   │ Adler,  Ronald        LOCALP0          Finance         │    │
│   │ Bolton, Raymond       LOCALPO          consultant      │    │
│   │ Castillo, Carlos      LOCALPO          Administration  │    │
│   │ Westland, Bob         LOCALPO          Marketing       │    │
│   │ Fraser, Abigail       LOCALPO          Marketing       │    │
│   │ Littler, Jerry        LOCALPO          Marketing       │    │
│   │ LOCALPO               FIRST555-8907                    │    │
│   │ FIRST                 9-6558-                          │    │
│   │                                                        │    │
│   └──────────────────────────────┴─────────────────────────┘    │
│                                                                   │
├──────────────────────────────────────────────────────────────────┤
│ Type new name and ENTER, ↑↓ and ENTER to select, F1 for help, Esc to end │
└──────────────────────────────────────────────────────────────────┘
```

Figure 10-7. cc:Mail Remote User directory

You are prompted:

Add new name or select existing name:

If you add a new name, it appears in the directory. If you select a name, you are placed in the Directory Menu:

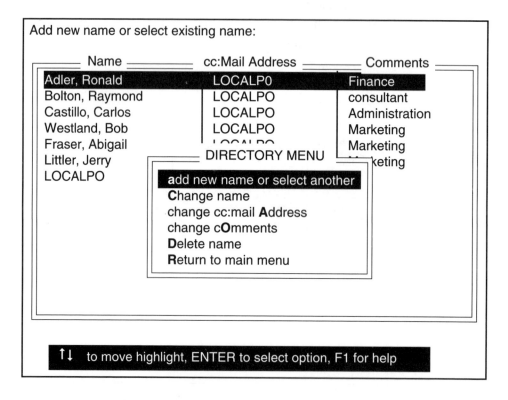

Figure 10-8. cc:Mail Remote Directory Menu

Three of the commands let you change the name, address, and comments field of the selected directory listing. If you select one of these options, you can edit the text in an editing field at the top of the screen. Two other commands let you delete the selected name or add new names to the directory.

Automatically Updating your Directory

You can update your directory automatically if your post office is running the optional cc:Mail Automatic Directory Exchange—which creates files of new names and changes and sends them to you. cc:Mail Remote recognizes these files and displays them with a **U** beside their Inbox listing.

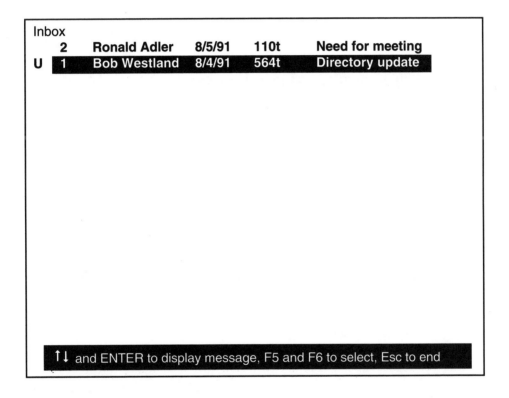

Figure 10-9. Inbox with U message

When you read an update message, you are placed in the Update Menu:

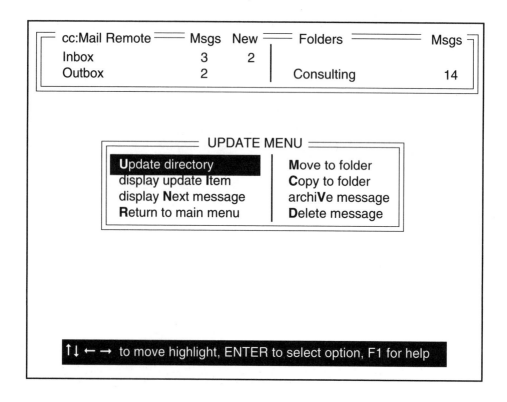

Figure 10-10. The Update Menu

After you read an update message, you can move the updated directory listing to a folder or your archives, or delete the update. To update the directory, select the "**U**pdate directory" command. You are prompted:

Are you sure you want to update your cc:Mail directory?

If you answer with a **Y**, your directory is updated. You can cancel the update by typing **N** or **Esc**.

Creating Address Strings and Script Files

You'll note in the directory example (Figure 10-7) that our fictional user, Raymond Bolton, uses LOCALPO as his home post office. You'll also note that LOCALPO has a phone number. Every user assigned to LOCALPO can be accessed by dialing the LOCALPO number.

Let's say that Raymond Bolton needs to dial a special billing sequence before long distance numbers. He can create a listing with the billing sequence, and then place the name of the listing in front of the phone number. (Figure 10-7 shows the billing sequence name dialing 9-6558 before the phone number.) This feature of cc:Mail Remote is particularly useful if you have a repetitive sequence to enter when your PC dials remote users of post offices. Instead of typing the sequence every time, name the sequence and list it in the address.

You may need to create a script file if you access a post office via a packet-switching network or an internal PBX switching system. Usually, your cc:Mail administrator will let you know if you need a script, and will generally send you one. If you use the word "script" in an address, cc:Mail Remote will use the script as the address. Enter the phone number after the word "script." Here is an example:

\ccmail\script 1-818-555-5697

Control commands, if required, are typed with the symbol ^. There are five script commands:

ATTN

Tells cc:Mail Remote to issue an attention or break signal.

DIAL

Tells cc:Mail Remote to dial the number that has been entered.

CCMAIL

Initiates the cc:Mail Remote communication protocol to connect to another cc:Mail system. This command is used at the end of the script that is connecting to another cc:Mail system.

HANGUP

Hangs up the telephone.

This section just touches on the basics of creating a script. Because this manual is a user guide, not a guide for administering a group of cc:Mail users, consult your cc:Mail administrator if you need to use a script and are having problems. In general, if you are using a regular telephone line, you will not need any special scripts.

Creating Mail

Chapter 5 and Appendices A and B provide detailed information on using the text and graphics editors. Briefly, however, you use cc:Mail Remote just like cc:Mail to create messages and attach files, except you use the Store Menu instead of the Send Menu. Since the local cc:Mail user agent operates on a LAN, the "Send message" command sends messages to a post office immediately.

cc:Mail Remote's Outbox stores multiple messages until you are ready to send them to the cc:Mail post office. If you are sending five to ten messages at a time, this will save a lot of money. You can edit or delete messages in the Outbox using the "reTrieve messages" option on the Main Menu.

Sending and Receiving Mail

Select the "Send/receive messages" command on the Main Menu to send messages:

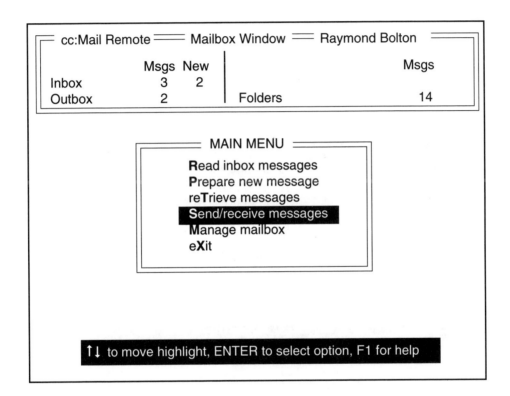

Figure 10-11. Main Menu with the Send/receive messages command.

Selecting the "Send/receive messages" command places you in the Send/
Receive Menu:

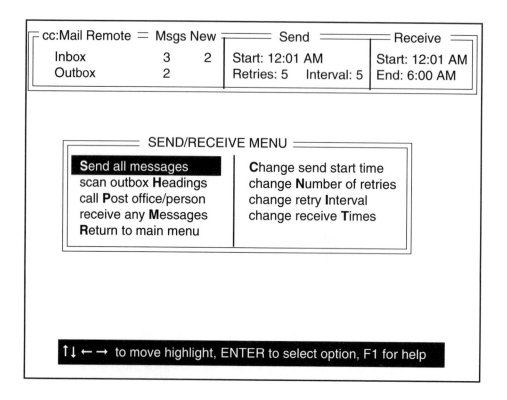

Figure 10-12. The Send/Receive Menu

The Send/Receive Menu can have up to nine commands. Six of the commands
are associated with sending messages:

- "Send all messages" sends all messages in the Outbox to as many different
  post offices and individual recipients as required.

- "scan outbox **Headings**" allows selected messages to be flagged for transmission.

- "call **P**ost office/person" transmits all messages in the Outbox addressed to a specific person or post office.

- "**C**hange send start time" allows you to set a time at which cc:Mail will begin sending the selected mail messages in its Outbox. You can set any time you wish, using standard AM/PM format, or the 24-hour clock. For example, type in 2PM as either 2:00PM or 14:00.

- "change **N**umber of retries" allows you to set the number of times cc:Mail Remote will retry a number if it cannot make a connection. cc:Mail can make up to 9,999 retries. A realistic number of retries is between five and ten.

- "change retry **I**nterval" allows you to set the interval between retries; it can be set as long as 1,440 minutes. A realistic interval is one to five minutes.

Two commands are associated with receiving messages:

- "receive any **M**essages" puts cc:Mail in its receive messages mode, in which it waits to be called by another cc:Mail Remote user or by a post office set up to deliver mail.

- "change receive **T**imes" determines the hours in which cc:Mail will be in host mode, waiting to answer its modem and exchange messages. Use standard AM/PM format, or the 24-hour clock. For example, type in 2PM as either 2:00PM or 14:00. If a Send start time is specified within a Host Receive mode range, cc:Mail will switch modes at the appropriate time to send messages, perform its tasks, and reset itself in waiting mode. This allows you to send and receive messages during a specified period, such as from midnight to 6AM, when rates are lower.

- The "**R**eturn to main menu" command returns you to the Main Menu.

Note: Whenever a cc:Mail Remote user connects to a post office or person, mail is typically exchanged in two directions. Mail in the Outbox is sent, while incoming mail is received. The only difference between "**S**end all messages" and "receive any **M**essages" is the order in which the exchange takes place: the Send command sends all messages to each location before receiving mail; the Receive command does the reverse. The only exception is if you set the S/O (send-only) or R/O (receive-only) option when you first ran cc:Mail Remote.

Sending Mail

When you select the "Send all messages" command, every message in the Outbox is sent. The recipients must have addresses in the cc:Mail directory. If a special start time is selected to send messages, the sending process will be held up until that time. To change the send start time, change "Change send start time" to "immediate."

When you select the "scan outbox **Headings**" command, your Outbox is listed. To send a message, select one and press **ENTER**. To send a group of messages, use **F5** and **F6** to select the beginning and end of a group, and press **ENTER**.

Use the "call **P**ost office/person" command to select messages in the Outbox addressed to a specific person or post office. This command sends only those messages in the Outbox addressed to a specific person or post office.

Note: When you are sending messages, make sure that the places where the messages are being received expect to hear from you; otherwise you will not be able to send messages.

Receiving Mail

The process of receiving messages is the reverse of sending them. When you use cc:Mail Remote, you log on and send messages, and then you receive incoming messages. When you are in the receive mode, other mail systems call you and log on, send messages, and receive messages from you. (They say it is better to give than to receive. In cc:Mail Remote, it is better to receive; the sender normally pays for the phone call!)

Send/Receive Status Information

cc:Mail Remote shows you the status of all transmissions on a step-by-step basis. It keeps the status on your screen until you press **ENTER**. If multiple calls are made or received, each call is treated as a transmission. Here is an example:

8/6/91 11:05AM   Placing call to LOCALPO.

Connection accepted.

2 messages sent.

1 message received.

8/6/91   11:08AM   Hanging up telephone. On hook.

Summary

cc:Mail Remote is a powerful program that lets people exchange electronic mail messages easily. cc:Mail Remote is particularly useful because it allows two people to connect directly, or hundreds of people to connect in a wide variety of ways. A system that begins with two people can grow to four or five, and can become a hub that serves as a central clearinghouse. Eventually, the hub can expand into a LAN node with dial-in capabilities.

USING CC: MAIL

CHAPTER 11

Error Messages for cc:Mail Remote

If personal computers were perfect . . . .

We all know they're not. As a result, a critical part of any program is how it handles errors when they occur. Many programs deliver esoteric messages that have meaning only to the programmer. We've all had experiences where a program has crashed and it says something like, "Error in module DC03:0B16."

cc:Mail Remote tries to give error messages in English, so that users will understand what the problem is. If you receive an error message while using cc:Mail Remote and cannot resolve the problem, contact your cc:Mail administrator. The error messages are:

Accepted r/o connection.
The person calling you is not in your directory. You must add the caller to your directory before calls can be accepted.

Address buffer full.
You have reached the address limit. To add more addressees to the message, you must send the message more than once.

Block cannot be copied into itself.
When editing a message, you create text blocks by pressing **F5** at the beginning of the block, and pressing **F6** at the end. You can copy this block of text by moving

the cursor to a position outside the block and pressing **Alt-F6**. You cannot press **Alt-F6** and copy the block of text inside itself.

Block cannot be moved into itself.

When editing a message, you create text blocks by pressing **F5** at the beginning of the block, and pressing **F6** at the end. You can move this block of text by moving the cursor to a position outside the block and pressing **Alt-F5**. You cannot press **Alt-F5** and move the block of text inside itself.

Connection refused.

You are attempting to call a cc:Mail host that has refused to make a connection because you supplied the wrong password. Check the password and try again.

Data connection not accepted.

The post office or remote system you called did not initiate the normal handshake routine. Have the administrator of the other system check to see that their system is set to receive and try again.

Data connection not established.

There was no data carrier at the remote system or post office being called. Have the administrator of the other system check to see that their system is set to receive and try again.

Data connection not requested.

The person calling your system did not initiate its calling sequence as your system requested. Have the administrator of the other system check to see that their system is set to send and try again.

Database drive/directory name too long.

The name of the cc:Mail database location exceeds the 23-character limit imposed by DOS. Notify your cc:Mail administrator to change the drive/directory name to a proper length.

Database file already locked.

cc:Mail has tried to lock a database file that is already locked. This error should not occur in normal operations and indicates a potentially serious problem. Contact your cc:Mail administrator.

Database file already unlocked.

cc:Mail has tried to unlock a database file that is already unlocked. This error should not occur in normal operations and indicates a potentially serious problem. Contact your cc:Mail administrator.

Database file cannot be accessed.

cc:Mail cannot access the cc:Mail database. This means there is some problem with the disk on the server or with the LAN. It could be as simple as the power being off, if the disk drive is separate from the operating system's drive. It could also indicate a serious problem with the hard drive. Check all hardware, reboot cc:Mail, and try to access the database again.

Database file cannot be found.

cc:Mail cannot find one of its database files on the cc:Mail server. The file may be damaged on the disk, or it may have been deleted.

Database file cannot be locked.

cc:Mail tried to lock a file and has not succeeded. This error should not occur in normal operations and indicates a potentially serious problem. Contact your cc:Mail administrator.

Database file cannot be unlocked.

cc:Mail tried to unlock a file and has not succeeded. This error should not occur in normal operations and indicates a potentially serious problem. Contact your cc:Mail administrator.

Database file cannot be opened.

cc:Mail tried to open a file and has not succeeded. Check your hardware to make certain the hard disk where the file resides is connected properly and is in operating condition.

Database file not locked.

cc:Mail expected to find a file that was locked, but it was unlocked. This error should not occur in normal operations and indicates a potentially serious problem. Contact your cc:Mail administrator.

Database file too large.

The cc:Mail database has an internal size limit set by the administrator. It has exceeded this size. This error should not occur in normal operations and indicates a potentially serious problem. Contact your cc:Mail administrator.

Database index out of range.

cc:Mail keeps an index of where all files are stored and lists its parameters within specific ranges. The database has stored a parameter that is out of its defined range. This error should not occur in normal operations and indicates a potentially serious problem. Contact your cc:Mail administrator.

Database page cannot be read correctly.

cc:Mail tried to read your hard drive, but could not. Check your hardware to make certain the hard disk where the file resides is connected properly and is in operating condition.

Database page cannot be written.

cc:Mail tried to read your hard drive, but could not. Check your hardware to make certain the hard disk where the file resides is connected properly and is in operating condition.

Database page cannot be read after write.

cc:Mail tried to read your hard drive, but could not. Check your hardware to make certain the hard disk where the file resides is connected properly and is in operating condition.

Database page read after write does not match.

cc:Mail tried to read your hard drive, but could not. Check your hardware to make certain the hard disk where the file resides is connected properly and is in operating condition.

Database pointer out of range.

cc:Mail tried to read your hard drive, but could not. Check your hardware to make certain the hard disk where the file resides is connected properly and is in operating condition.

Dates must be entered as mm/dd/yy.

cc:Mail uses the numeric format of month/day/year, such as 12/31/91 (December 31, 1991). Enter the date with the correct format.

Disk error in archiving message.

An error occurred trying to copy your message to an archive file. Try copying the message again to the same archive file and to another archive file. If you cannot do either, it means that the message or both files are damaged.

Disk error in attaching file.

An error occurred trying to attach a DOS item to a file. The item cannot be attached to a cc:Mail message.

Disk error in copying item.

An error occurred trying to copy a cc:Mail item to a file. Try using another drive and/or directory.

Disk error in reading file.

An error occurred trying to read a file into a text item. The file is damaged and cannot be read into a cc:Mail message.

Disk error in writing message.

An error occurred while the message was being written to an ASCII file. Try the operation using another drive and/or directory to see whether the message is damaged, or whether there was a problem writing to the drive/directory.

Drive cannot be accessed.

The drive letter is unknown or there is no disk in a floppy drive. Recheck your drive specification and make sure a diskette is available.

Duplicate name in directory.

You entered a name in the directory that already exists. You cannot have duplicate names, so either escape from the sequence or change the name you're entering.

Error in ALT command line parameter.

cc:Mail allows you to use the **Alt** key with another key, such as **Alt-2** or **Alt-F1**, to perform specific commands. You have used an **Alt-x** combination that cannot be used at this point in the program. Study the documentation or ask your cc:Mail administrator to find the correct command.

Error in MSGSIZE/n command line parameter.

You have entered a MSGSIZE/n parameter that exceeds its maximum size of 24 (24 Kbytes).

Error in RECLAIM/n command line parameter.

You have entered a RECLAIM/n parameter that exceeds its maximum size of 64 (64 Kbytes).

Error in script file line.

There is an error in the script you wrote to access a cc:Mail Remote system.

File cannot be found.

You have specified a file name that does not exist on that drive and directory. Retype the name.

File does not have archive format.

You have selected an archive file for a message that does not have cc:Mail's archive format. Select a correct archive file or contact your cc:Mail administrator if you believe that you have selected a correct archive file.

File is not a text Snapshot.

You have selected a file to be read into the text editor that is supposed to be a text Snapshot, but is in a graphics or binary format and cannot be read into the editor.

File item cannot be read.

The file item you have selected to be displayed cannot be read because it is damaged.

File with that name cannot be created.

You have selected a name for a file that does not adhere to DOS conventions. Try another name that falls within the DOS parameter of XXXXXXXX.XXX.

Folder disk must be in drive B.

You have tried to access a folder on drive B: (a floppy drive), but the diskette in the drive does not contain that folder. Insert the correct disk and try again.

Folder not found.

You have specified a folder name that does not match any folders you have stored in cc:Mail. Try the name again. Contact your cc:Mail administrator if you know you've created a folder and cc:Mail cannot find it.

Graphic item cannot be displayed.

You have selected a graphics item to be displayed or inserted into the graphics editor, but your PC does not have a graphics monitor available.

Graphic item cannot be read.

You have selected a graphics item to be displayed or inserted into the graphics editor that cannot be read because the file is damaged.

Graphic Snapshot cannot be displayed.

You have selected a graphics Snapshot file to be displayed or inserted into the graphics editor, but your PC does not have a graphics monitor available.

Help file cannot be found.

The file Mail.help is not on the drive and directory in which the cc:Mail post office is located. Contact your cc:Mail administrator.

Help screen cannot be read.

The help file at your cc:Mail post office is damaged. Contact your cc:Mail administrator.

Incompatible database.

cc:Mail separates its database from the LAN program and keeps track of program versions for both. You have a database version that does not work with the LAN program version. To solve the problem, you must upgrade your software properly. Contact your cc:Mail administrator.

Incorrect number of command-line parameters.

When you are starting up cc:Mail, you access the program with a command line that defines who you are and where the program is located. You have not provided enough information in your command line to access cc:Mail correctly. Reenter the command line. Contact your cc:Mail administrator if you have trouble accessing cc:Mail.

Incorrect priority level.

The priority level you have entered is incorrect. It must be a U, N, or L. Reenter the priority level.

Insufficient disk space.

There are three conditions in which this message will be given. First, your Mailbox diskette does not have enough space to store a message being received. Second, the remote PC you are sending to does not have enough disk space to store the message you have sent. Third, you do not have enough disk space to reorganize your cc:Mail database and reclaim free space. In all three cases, messages must be deleted to free up more space.

Insufficient disk space for database file.

cc:Mail allocates a certain amount of space for the database file. The size has been exceeded. More space must be allocated to the database file.

Insufficient disk space to copy item.

You have run out of disk space at your server.

Insufficient disk space to copy message.

You have run out of disk space at your server.

Insufficient disk space to create dos file.

You have run out of disk space on the drive you specified to create your DOS file. Use a new disk or erase files from the one you specified.

Insufficient disk space to create item.

You have run out of disk space at your server and cannot create a new item. Notify your cc:Mail administrator. To save the item in the interim, write the text to a DOS file or take a Snapshot of the screen if it is a graphics item.

Insufficient disk space to store message.

You have run out of disk space at your server and cannot store the message. On an interim basis, write your text to a DOS file on a floppy disk, so it can be reloaded into a message later.

Insufficient disk space to store message in folder.

You have run out of disk space at your server and cannot store the message. On an interim basis, write your text to a DOS file on a floppy disk so it can be reloaded into a message later, or save it to a folder on a floppy diskette.

Insufficient disk space to store message in mailbox.

You have run out of disk space at your server and cannot store the message. On an interim basis, write your text to a DOS file on a floppy disk so it can be reloaded into a message later, or save it to a folder on a floppy diskette.

Insufficient disk space to write file.

You have run out of disk space on the disk you have specified. Erase files from the disk or use another one.

Insufficient memory.

You need 84K to run cc:Mail. Either free memory from your PC or add more.

Insufficient space in text buffer.

There is not enough space in your text buffer to perform the requested editing operation. Save the buffer and write a block into another item to perform your desired task.

Invalid cc:Mail address.

The address you entered matches an address in the directory, but is not defined as a post office. Change the entry to a P for post office.

Item cannot be displayed.

You have specified an item that your PC cannot display; for example, you have specified a graphics item and your PC does not have a graphics card.

Item cannot be read.

You have specified an item that is damaged and cannot be read by cc:Mail. Request that the sender check the item and resend a clean copy.

Line number out of range.

cc:Mail allows you to enter a specific range of lines from an ASCII file into the text editor, so that you only load a portion of the file. The line numbers must be positive integers. You have specified incorrect line numbers, such as a number larger than the total number in the file. Keep in mind that a line is defined as a RETURN stored in the file.

Line will be too long after replacing.

Setting your margin to 80 characters disables word wrap; you have requested a search-and-replace operation that will exceed the 80-character limit. Reformat the line so the operation can be performed.

Mail password not correct.

You have specified a password that is not correct. Try it again. Notify your cc:Mail administrator if there is a problem.

Message buffer full.

You have attempted to retrieve a large number of messages at the same time and the message buffer has filled up. Try retrieving a smaller number of messages.

Message cannot be copied.

A disk error occurred while the message was being copied to a folder at the server. Try the function again. If the problem still exists, contact your cc:Mail administrator.

Message cannot be delivered.

A disk error occurred while you were trying to deliver a message. Try again to deliver the message.

Message cannot be moved.

A disk error occurred while you were moving a message. Try again if the message has not been damaged.

Message cannot be read.

The message you are trying to access is damaged and cannot be read.

Message cannot be read. Entry deleted.

The message you are trying to access is damaged and cannot be read. It will be deleted.

Message cannot be stored.

A disk error occurred while you were storing a message. The message has not been stored.

Message item cannot be copied.

A disk error occurred while you were trying to copy a message item. The item may be damaged or the temporary file used cannot be created.

Message numbers must be entered as 1,3,5-8,10 for example.

When using the command line to type in a command associated with messages, you must use commas to delineate single messages and a dash to delineate a range. The numbers you typed could not be interpreted.

Message recipients not in mail directory.

You have sent a message (or messages) to a post office and the names specified were not in that directory.

Message size too long.

You have sent a message (or messages) to a post office that has a maximum size for a message and you have exceeded that maximum.

Modem not responding.

.   Your modem is not responding. Check all hardware connections and make sure that you have specified the appropriate COM port.

Name may not be post office.

You have entered a name that is listed as a post office. Enter a different name.

New database file cannot be created.

A new database file could not be created during a Reclaim operation. Make sure you have read/write privileges and enough space on your hard disk.

New titles may not be entered.

You have used up the maximum 200 folders and/or private mailing lists that you can stored in cc:Mail, and you cannot create a new one until one or more of the old ones is deleted.

No more characters may be entered.

You have entered more characters than you are allowed. Retry your entry with fewer characters.

Not all files are displayed.

You have asked to see a listing of directory files and there are more files in the directory than cc:Mail displays. Enter the specific file you want to see, or use a * with some descriptive information to see a subset that will display your file.

Page table full.

cc:Mail keeps an internal page table that has become full. This error should not occur in normal operations and indicates a potentially serious problem. Contact your cc:Mail administrator.

Phrase not found.

When editing text, you have asked to find a phrase that is not in the text.

Please type Y for Yes, or ENTER or N for No.

You were asked for a Y, N, or ENTER response and did not provide one. Type in one of the three responses.

Printer is unavailable.

You want to print a message or file and your printer is not available. Check to make sure the printer is connected properly and turned on, and retry the command. If you still have a problem, make sure the printer is set up to print on the same LPTx channel as you specified to cc:Mail. The default is LPT1.

Requested wrong name.

You have tried to log on to a system that is using another name. Call to find the correct name and try again.

R/O connection accepted.

Your name is not listed in the mail directory at the remote system you attempted to access. Have your name entered and try again.

Script file cannot be found.

You have tried to log on to a system using a script file that cannot be located. Specify the correct name and pathway to the file and try again.

Serial port not responding.

The serial port is not responding. Try entering a new port after rechecking the port configuration.

Snapshot cannot be read.

You have requested that cc:Mail create an item that is labeled a snapshot. The file does not appear to be a snapshot. Select the appropriate file or retake the snapshot and retry the command.

Still off-hook.

The modem cannot hang up the telephone. Reset the modem manually.

Telephone number not available.

You have tried to log on to a system, but have not specified a phone number. Enter the phone number and try again.

Text buffer full.

You have filled your text buffer with 20,000 characters. To continue, you must end the item and start a new one, or copy the item to a file and delete half of it, so you have two items of about 10,000 characters each.

Text item cannot be read.

You have requested that cc:Mail access a text item that cannot be read properly. The item is damaged.

Time must be entered as hh:mm and AM or PM.

You have entered a time with an incorrect format.

Unable to accept data call.

The system calling yours was not able to establish a data link. cc:Mail will reset the modem to wait for another call.

Unable to accept voice call.

The system calling yours was not able to establish a data link. Most likely someone was attempting a voice call. cc:Mail will reset the modem to wait for another call.

Undeliverable update file.

The update file CCMUDAT.UND cannot be created because there is not enough space on the hard disk.

Unknown recipients.

You are either receiving messages for people who are not listed in your directory, or sending messages to people not listed in the directory at the receiving system. The message(s) could not be delivered to the specified addressee(s).

Warning: Multiple attempts needed to read database page.

There is a hardware problem with access to your hard disk, controller or RAM. Check your hardware.

Warning: Multiple attempts needed to write database page.

There is a hardware problem with access to your hard disk, controller, or RAM. Check your hardware.

Wrong name requested.

The calling system has the wrong name associated with the address in your directory. Make sure the administrator at the calling system has the names entered correctly.

cc:Mail for The Macintosh

USING CC: MAIL

CHAPTER 12

Installing cc:Mail on Macintosh Computers

This chapter explains how to install cc:Mail on your Macintosh computer. It assumes that your cc:Mail administrator has set up a mailbox for you at a nearby cc:Mail post office and, furthermore, that you are already set up on a local area network (LAN), such as AppleTalk or Ethernet.

LAN Basics

The key point to understand about a LAN is that it provides communications between a server device that houses specific programs and/or data files and the client computer that accesses those files via the LAN. In an AppleTalk LAN that operates the AppleShare server software, for example, the client will be any Macintosh on the LAN, while the server will be the specific machine that houses the AppleShare LAN server software. In the TOPS LAN that is also popular in Macintosh environments, the user of any computer can act as a server by "publishing" specific folders that may be accessed by other users.

To access a LAN server, the user goes out over the communications network and looks into specific available disks, as illustrated by the following example of a TOPS network:

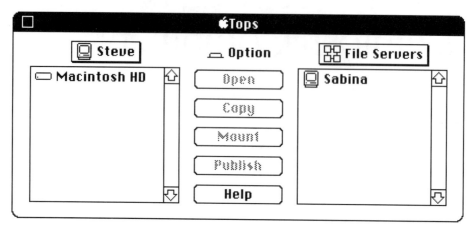

Figure 12-1. A TOPS network

The local Macintosh is named Steve and the server is named Sabina. If Steve clicks on the Sabina file server, it will open as if it were a regular Macintosh file. It can even be mounted on Steve's desktop under Finder, which is shown in the following example:

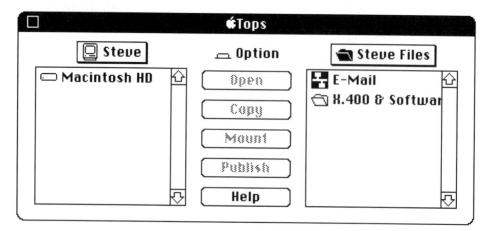

Figure 12-2. A TOPS network with E-Mail folder

When the e-mail folder is mounted, it appears on the desktop under Finder as if it were a local floppy disk, as shown below:

Figure 12-3. The e-mail folder appears as a local floppy disk

Operating under a LAN in the Macintosh environment is completely transparent to the user. When you open your e-mail folder, there is no indication that the folder actually resides on a different computer, as shown below:

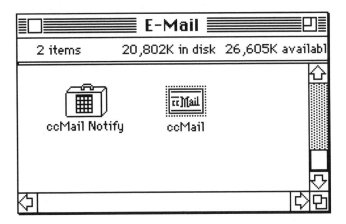

Figure 12-4. The e-mail folder appears as a resident folder

Macintosh User Requirements

In order to install cc:Mail properly, your Macintosh must have:

* 1 megabyte of RAM and 128K ROMs, which is available with all Macintosh Pluses, SEs, Classics, and Macintosh II computers. If your Macintosh has 128K of RAM or 512K of RAM, it will most likely have to be upgraded to run cc:Mail.

* Macintosh operating system version 6.0.2 version or later. To see which version of the operating system is running on your Macintosh and how much memory you have, move to the Macintosh desktop, click on the Apple icon in the right hand corner of the screen, and drag down to the **About The Finder** command. If your system does not say 6.0.2 or higher, you cannot run cc:Mail. Incidentally, if you click on the Apple icon and the first command line does not say **About The Finder**, but instead says **About** some other program, you are *not* at the Macintosh desktop. Select the **Quit** command from the **File** Menu to return to the desktop.

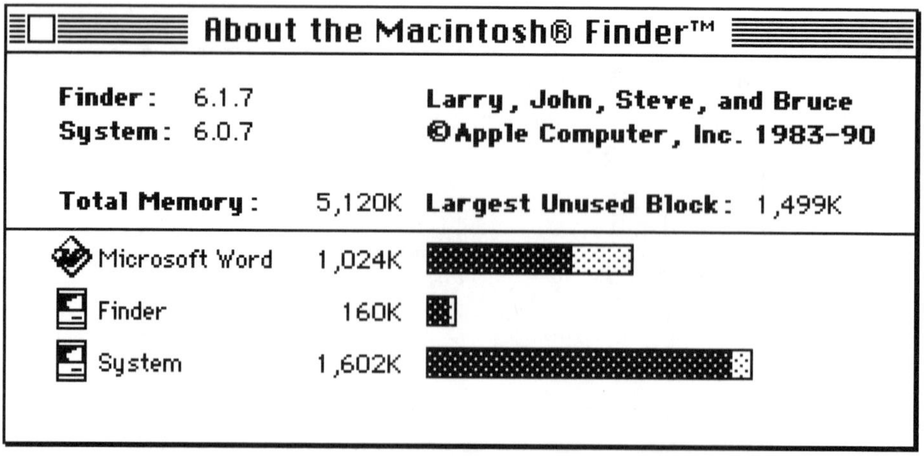

```
┌──────────────────────────────────────────────────┐
│ ▤▭▭▭▭ About the Macintosh® Finder™ ▭▭▭▭ │
├──────────────────────────────────────────────────┤
│ Finder:   6.1.7          Larry, John, Steve, and Bruce │
│ System:   6.0.7          ©Apple Computer, Inc. 1983–90 │
│                                                    │
│ Total Memory:   5,120K  Largest Unused Block: 1,499K │
├──────────────────────────────────────────────────┤
│ ◆ Microsoft Word   1,024K  ▓▓▓▓▓▓░░░              │
│ ▤ Finder             160K  ▓                      │
│ ▤ System           1,602K  ▓▓▓▓▓▓▓▓▓▓▓▓▓░         │
└──────────────────────────────────────────────────┘
```

Figure 12-5. *About The Finder* tells you which version of the Macintosh operating system you are running.

- An AppleTalk-compatible LAN and a server that is running the AppleShare
  file server protocol (AFP). Since this manual is about using cc:Mail (not
  setting cc:Mail up on a LAN) we assume that you have the appropriate LAN
  environment. For more information on setting up cc:Mail, consult the
  companion book to this user's guide, Eric Arnum's *Delivering cc:Mail* (M&T
  Books, 1991).

Installing the cc:Mail User Programs

Each cc:Mail user should have two programs on their computer: the cc:Mail
program file and the cc:Mail Notify desktop accessory. These programs will be
provided to you by your cc:Mail administrator either on a floppy disk or in a folder
on your network's server. To install the program, you must copy these files to your
Macintosh and then install the Notify desktop accessory in your system folder.

For the purposes of this book, we will assume that you have the cc:Mail folder
mounted. To install cc:Mail, create a folder for cc:Mail using the **New Folder**
command from the **File** Menu. You can name the folder anything you want. Open
the e-mail folder mounted on the server (or double-click on the floppy disk icon) and
click on both the cc:Mail and Notify icons, as shown:

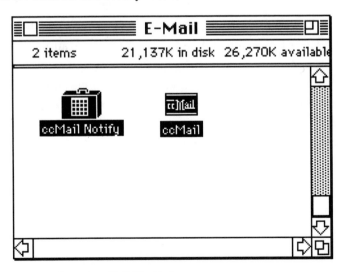

Figure 12-6. The cc:Mail and cc:Mail Notify icons

After selecting both files, drag the icons to the new folder that you have created. Your Macintosh will copy the files onto your disk. When you run cc:Mail, you will open the cc:Mail program in the folder you have created.

After you have copied the cc:Mail and cc:Mail Notify programs, close the e-mail directory and drag the directory icon (or the cc:Mail floppy disk icon) to the Trash Can. This will dismount the directory from your desktop and close the connection between your Macintosh and the file server. Don't worry about closing this connection. When operating on a LAN, you want to use resources only when required. When you use cc:Mail, you will reestablish the connection between your Macintosh and the server.

Launching cc:Mail the First Time

Since cc:Mail is a network program, it must access the network server to check your Inbox, send messages, or perform almost any other task. This means that the network and the cc:Mail server must both be operational. In the Macintosh environment, you can find out if the basic AppleTalk network is active by selecting **Chooser** from the **Apple** Menu. A window with printer and network options will appear; make sure that AppleTalk shows as active.

You also must know the specific server, and folder on the server, before you can launch cc:Mail, as well as the initial user ID and password that has been set up for you. If you don't have this information yet, contact your cc:Mail administrator before continuing.

The first time you launch cc:Mail, your server volume (folder) containing the post office database must be mounted on the Macintosh desktop as described above. In cc:Mail prior to Version 1.20, the server must remain mounted at all times. In Version 1.20, the server need not be mounted after the first time.

Selecting a Post Office

To open up cc:Mail for the first time, double-click on the cc:Mail icon in your folder. You will be asked to select a post office:

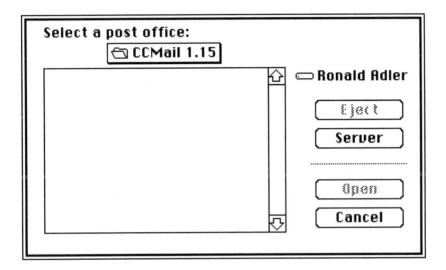

Figure 12-7. A post office window

Click on the **Server** button until you find the server that houses the post office. When you have found the server, double-click on it. Next, find the directory that has the cc:Mail post office, which is labeled cc:Mail™. Double-click on the cc:Mail™ icon as shown:

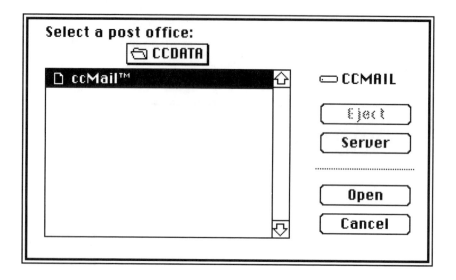

Figure 12-8. cc:Mail™ selected

Logging on to cc:Mail

When you double-click on the cc:Mail icon, it will show you the log-in screen as shown:

```
┌─────────────────────────────────────────┐
│                                           │
│        ┌─ Welcome to ccMail ─┐            │
│                                           │
│   Name:    ┌──────────────────────────┐   │
│            │                          │   │
│            └──────────────────────────┘   │
│   Password: ┌─────────────────────────┐   │
│             │                         │   │
│             └─────────────────────────┘   │
│                                           │
│        ( Quit )      ( OK )               │
│                                           │
└─────────────────────────────────────────┘
```

Figure 12-9. The log-in screen

Type in your name and password exactly as they were given to you. The first time you log on, if a password has not been assigned to you, whatever you type in the Password field will become your new password. You must type your user name and password every time you enter cc:Mail. You will then see the main cc:Mail screen:

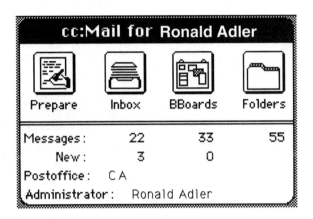

Figure 12-10. The main cc:Mail screen

A Word on Your Password

While the password may seem a bit like playing cloak and dagger, it is the only thing that stands between you and open access to your files. All of cc:Mail's files are on a central server. When you log on, you tell the server who you are with a name and password. Your name is listed in the cc:Mail directory so that everyone knows it; if anyone knows your password, they can log on as you and read all of your mail.

If a password has been assigned to you, it is probably designed to be easy to remember. When you enter cc:Mail for the first time, the first thing you should do is change your password.

There is something of a science to passwords, actually; "hackers" try to break into IDs illegally by guessing passwords. They do it by choosing obvious numbers or names, such as birthdays or the names of a husband, wife, or child.

When you choose your password, make it something that has no logical connection to you, but is easy to remember. It can be up to ten characters. One good choice is the PIN number for your bank automated teller machine, assuming that you keep this number private. You might also choose your favorite number or some random combination of letters that has no meaning for anyone except you.

To change your password, open the Admin Menu and select the **Change Password** command. You will be prompted to enter your old password to confirm your identity and then to enter your new password twice to confirm that it is correct.

If You Forget Your Password

If you forget your password, you cannot access your mailbox. Your cc:Mail administrator can, however, erase your password and create a new one for you, so that you can gain access to the account again. Remember: only your cc:Mail administrator can do this.

Using cc:Mail Again

When you use cc:Mail the first time, it creates a special icon in your cc:Mail folder, with the same name as your post office. It contains the pathway to access your local server and your cc:Mail name. The icon looks like this:

Figure 12-11. The local cc:Mail icon

In the future, log on to cc:Mail by double-clicking this icon. It will automatically connect you to the cc:Mail server and request your password. You can drag this icon to your desktop if you want.

Installing the Notify Desk Accessory

One of the programs you copy when you install cc:Mail is cc:Mail Notify, with an icon that looks like a suitcase. The program is a desktop accessory (DA), which means that it can pop up and run over other programs in its own window. Periodically, the Notify DA checks with your cc:Mail server to see if you have any new mail. (The checking is done in background, so you don't even know it is taking place.) You are notified when you have messages, based on the parameters you have selected.

To install cc:Mail Notify, use the Font/DA Mover program included with your Macintosh system to copy it as a desktop accessory into your system file. (Refer to your Macintosh documentation if you do not know how to use the Font/DA Mover.) When you open the Font/DA Mover program, you must open up the Notify suitcase icon and the system file. Then select the Notify program and copy it into the system file as shown below:

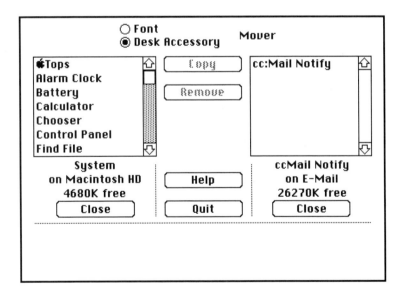

Figure 12-12. Installing cc:Mail Notify

Once the DA is installed, it will appear in the **Apple** ✿ Menu under the name cc:Mail Notify. Before the Notify utility will work, it must be set up properly. Select the cc:Mail Notify DA by dragging the cursor to it in the **Apple** ✿ Menu and releasing the mouse button. The following window pops up:

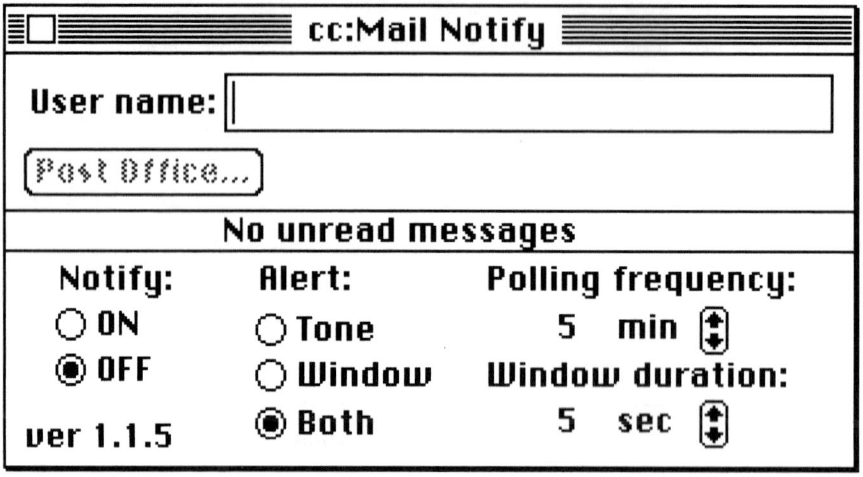

```
┌───────────────────────────────────────────────┐
│ ▤☐▤▤▤▤▤▤▤▤▤▤  cc:Mail Notify  ▤▤▤▤▤▤▤▤▤▤▤▤ │
├───────────────────────────────────────────────┤
│  User name: │                               │ │
│             └───────────────────────────────┘ │
│  ┌─────────────┐                              │
│  │ Post Office...│                            │
│  └─────────────┘                              │
├───────────────────────────────────────────────┤
│              No unread messages                │
├───────────────────────────────────────────────┤
│  Notify:      Alert:      Polling frequency:   │
│  ○ ON         ○ Tone          5   min  ⬍       │
│  ◉ OFF        ○ Window    Window duration:      │
│  ver 1.1.5    ◉ Both          5   sec  ⬍       │
└───────────────────────────────────────────────┘
```

Figure 12-13. Setting up the Notify options

You must give cc:Mail Notify the server and folder location for your post office, just as you did for the main cc:Mail program. After you have done this, select whether you want the Notify capability **On** or **Off** by clicking on the appropriate button. You must also select whether you want a tone alert, a window to pop up, or both. If you select both, the Alert sound will be invoked by your system, and you'll see a message in the upper-right corner of your screen telling you how many new messages you have.

CHAPTER 13

Overview of cc:Mail for the Macintosh

After you double-click the cc:Mail icon on your desktop and enter your ID and password, you will be in cc:Mail's main window (also called the Control Panel) as shown below.

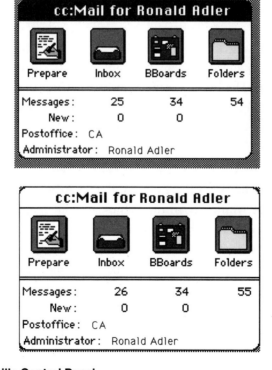

Figure 13-1. cc:Mail's Control Panel

cc:Mail's Control Panel provides four buttons and four menus.

Buttons:

- Prepare, for creating new messages

- Inbox, for reading your mail

- BBoards, for reading and posting to bulletin boards

- Folders, for saving and retrieving messages

Menus:

- File, for creating and saving documents and folders

- Edit, for editing text

- Mail, for using mail, folders, bulletin boards, and archives

- Admin, (or Special) for changing your password and creating mailing lists

You may have to adjust to using cc:Mail's buttons. Icons inside cc:Mail are buttons, not file icons. The buttons on the Control Panel perform their functions when you click on them once, and the buttons in the message window have drop-down menus.

The Menus

cc:Mail has four menus: **File**, **Edit**, **Mail,** and **Admin**. When you first enter cc:Mail, only the **File, Mail,** and **Admin** Menus are available. The **File** Menu is also used to create and save documents, print messages, and quit the program. The **Edit** Menu operates only when you are creating messages. **Mail** duplicates the function of the buttons on the Control Panel, and adds commands for managing archives. **Admin** replaces the **Special** menu in earlier versions of the program.

File Menu

The File Menu includes these commands:

New   ⌘N

Open...   ⌘O

Open <document>

Close   ⌘W

Close All

Save   ⌘S

Save As

Page Setup ...

Print   ⌘P

Quit   ⌘Q

These are all standard Macintosh commands. If you use any Mac programs, you'll almost certainly know these commands—although you may not know the context in which they're used within cc:Mail.

The **New <document>** command is used to create a new folder when you are in your folder system, or new mailing lists in the mailing list window.

The **Open** command opens the selected item. The command is available when you first select a specific message. You can also open an item by double-clicking.

The **Open <document>** command opens the selected document. The name of the command changes depending upon the window you are in. For example, when bulletin boards are open, the command is shown as **Open Bulletin Board**. The command changes to **Folder, Bulletin Board, Message,** and **Item**. You can also double-click objects you want to open.

The **Close** and **Close All** commands close windows. You can also click on the close box in the window's top left hand corner, or use the short-cut ⌘ W.

The **Save** command saves the current item under its current name on its disk drive. New items are named "Untitled" and should be saved with the **Save As** command.

The **Save As** command opens the usual Macintosh dialog box for naming a file and choosing a volume and folder to save it in. Use the command the first time you save a document to give it a name other than "Untitled." **Save As** can also be used to save an item attached to a cc:Mail message as a separate file.

The **Page Setup** pulls up standard Macintosh dialog boxes for setting up a page for printing. The **Print** command prints a message.

The Edit Menu

The **Edit** Menu contains the standard Macintosh editing commands. You use editing commands in cc:Mail when creating messages or reading incoming messages. Cutting or copying information in cc:Mail stores it in the Macintosh clipboard. You can paste information from the clipboard into a message, the Scrapbook, or into another Macintosh program. The **Edit** menu has the following commands:

Undo   ⌘ Z

Cut   ⌘ X

Copy   ⌘ C

Paste   ⌘ V

Clear   ⌘ K

Select All ⌘ A

The **Undo** command is inactive in cc:Mail. Only **Copy** and **Select All** are available in Inbox messages.

The **Cut** command removes selected information from your message and puts it in the clipboard. The selected information is deleted from your message.

The **Copy** command copies selected information from your message and puts it in the clipboard. The selected information is not deleted from your message.

The **Paste** command inserts information in the clipboard into your document at the cursor location. **Paste** operates only from within the editor, although it is possible to copy information from any cc:Mail message and to paste it into another Macintosh program.

The **Clear** command deletes selected information from your document, but does not put it in the clipboard. (It works just like the **Backspace** key.) The **Clear** command is used to delete information from within a message item and does not work on overall messages or folders.

The **Select All** command selects everything in the active window. Once you have selected the objects, they can be opened, cut, copied, or cleared.

The Mail Menu

The Mail Menu is an alternate set of commands for the buttons on the Control Panel, along with a few other commands:

Prepare message only ⌘ M

Inbasket ⌘ I

Bulletin boards ⌘ B

Folders ⌘ F

Open archives...

Save as archive...

The first four commands duplicate the Control Panel buttons. You probably won't use them very much: it is easier to use a mouse or the command-key commands, such as ⌘ M or ⌘ I. The **Open archives** and **Save as archive** commands are used to save messages to your local PC or to the network. cc:Mail operates in a central server environment. All messages stored in your Inbasket or in a bulletin board or folder are stored on the server. The archives allow you to keep copies of messages on your own disks—either hard disk or floppy diskette, or on the network to an assigned volume or folder.

The Admin or Special Menus

The **Admin** Menu has two options: **Change Password** and **Mailing Lists**. **Change Password** asks you to enter your current password, and a new password. It displays the new password in plain text so you can confirm that you entered it correctly. The **Mailing Lists** command allows you to create private mailing lists. The lists appear in a mailing list directory that you can access when addressing messages.

Older versions of cc:Mail have a **Special** menu with only one command: **Change Password**. When you select this command, you are asked to enter your current password; you are then asked to enter your new password twice to make certain it is entered properly.

Summary

cc:Mail is very easy to use. A cc:Mail message consists of up to 20 items; each item comprises a block of text of up to 20,000 characters, a graphics item up to one screen in size, or a computer file. Messages are sent by the users on the system. Incoming messages are initially stored in your Inbasket. After you've read them, you can keep them in the Inbasket, move them to a folder on the server, and/or store them on a disk.

Logging on to cc:Mail places you in the Control Panel, where you can click on buttons to show the messages in your Inbasket, folders, or bulletin boards. You can also click on a button to prepare a message.

CHAPTER 14

Reading Messages on the Macintosh

Using cc:Mail or any e-mail system is similar to reading messages in your inbox on your desk. Imagine that you just sat down at your desk and pulled the top memo from your inbox. It's a message from your boss:

We will have a staff meeting next Wednesday at 9 a.m. in conference room 101. Please let me know if you have any conflict in attending, and also notify your staff that they should either attend or let my secretary know they cannot attend.

At this point, you would decide whether to reply to the memo and/or forward it to others. Then you'd decide whether to save or discard the memo itself. In the example above, you'd probably forward copies to your staff and send the original back to your boss with a reply saying whether or not you could attend. With an e-mail system, you can accomplish with a few simple commands on the computer what might take several sheets of paper and trips to the copy machine to accomplish in paper form.

Opening the Inbox

To read new messages in cc:Mail, click on the Inbox button in the cc:Mail application or select Inbox from the **Mail** Menu (or use the ⌘ I shortcut). Messages are listed in the Inbox with:

- The name of the sender

- The date sent

- The size of the message in stored bytes

- The type of message (t = text, f = file, g = graphics, x = fax)

- The subject of the message

Messages that have not been read appear in bold, while messages that have been read are in regular text format. A tiny white icon designates messages that have not been read, while a darker icon designates messages that have been read.

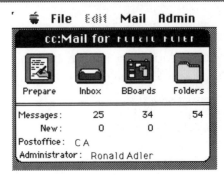

Figure 14-1. A cc:mail inbox listing.

To open a message, double-click on it, or click on it and select the **Open Message** (⌘ O) command from the **File** Menu. You can select more than one message by holding down the **Shift** key and clicking once on each message you want to open, then double-click on one of the messages or select **Open Messages** (⌘O) from the **File** Menu. As each message window closes, the previous message appears in its own window.

Message-Handling Buttons

The top of each message window shows the message number, and the date and time sent. The following eight buttons also appear at the top of the window, although only five are active:

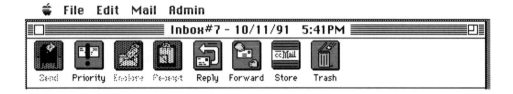

Figure 14-2. The message-handling buttons

The buttons represent actions you can take with your messages. The **Send, Enclose,** and **Receipt** buttons are associated with replying to or forwarding messages. They are active only after you have selected the **Reply** or **Forward** commands. When you are reading a message, the **Send, Enclose,** and **Receipt** buttons are not active.

The **Reply, Forward, Store,** and **Trash** commands work with messages that have been sent to you. Each command can be selected in sequence. It is quite common, for example, to reply to the sender of the message, forward copies to other people, and either store the message in another folder or put the message in the trash.

Reading Messages

Text messages

Most messages you receive will be text only and will not include any attachments. When you receive a text-only message, the text appears in the message window. Use the up and down arrows, the scroll box, or the scroll bar to scroll through the message.

You can move the window by clicking on the title bar and dragging it to a new location on the screen. You can increase or decrease the size of the window by clicking on the size box and dragging it to the size you want; double-click on the size box to return the window to its standard size.

After reading a text message, you can **Reply**, **Forward**, **Store**, **Trash**, or **Close** it.

Multi-item messages

cc:Mail allows you to enclose files in your messages as attachments. This means that you can share spreadsheets, graphics, formatted documents, and sounds with other users on your cc:Mail system. Messages with multiple items are slightly different than messages with only one item. The contents of a message with a single item are displayed automatically, while the contents of a multi-item message are displayed as file icons inside a typical Macintosh folder. If your message contains items other than the text of the message itself, the message and enclosed items appear as icons inside the message:

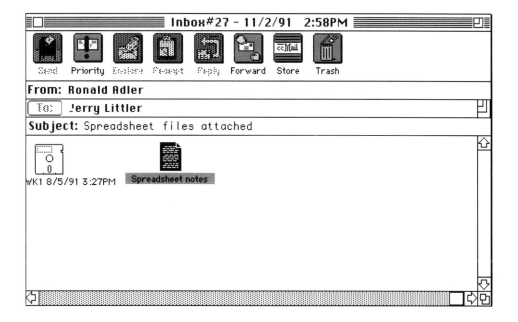

Figure 14-3. A multi-item message

There are two ways to examine the contents of an attached item.

If you double-click on an item, or select an item by clicking once and then selecting the **Open** command from the **File** Menu, the item opens in a separate window. When you close the window, you return to the message to which the item was attached. When you select an item that is a computer file, such as a file from a spreadsheet or word processing program, it will be displayed in cc:Mail in a read-only mode without specific typefaces and formats.

To open an item in the application it was created for (to open a spreadsheet in Excel, for example), click on the item and select **Save** or **Save As** from the File Menu and save the file to a folder on your desktop. You will then be able to open the file in its application.

cc:Mail has a unique feature for fax items in a message. When you open a fax item, you can press the plus key (+) to enlarge the image on the screen up to eight times its original size, or press the minus key (-) to reduce the image up to eight times. At any point, you can press the equal key (=) to return the image to its original size.

cc:Mail lets you do more than just send messages; you can send computer files, including programs and working files. To give an example of a potential application, many large firms have site licenses for their key software programs. cc:Mail can be used to distribute new releases of software electronically by sending the new program as an attached file to a return receipt message. With a return receipt, the sender knows who has read the message and, presumably, received the new release.

Replying to Messages

You have two choices when replying to a message. Do you send your reply to the sender only, or to all recipients of the message—and do you include a copy of the original message in your reply? Click on the Reply button and hold down the button on the mouse. Then drag down and select one of the following options:

To sender

To all

Message to sender

Message to all

Selecting **To sender** creates a blank reply for you to use to respond to the sender. (The attachments to the original message are not included in the reply.) The **To all** command sends a reply to the sender and all of the original recipients. (The attachments to the original message are not included in the reply.) The **Message to sender** command sends a reply with the attachments to the original message to the sender. The **Message to all** command sends a reply with the attachments to the original message to the sender and all of the original recipients.

cc:Mail saves attachments only once. This means that you can include a large number of attachments from the original message in your reply without taking up extra space on the disk. Imagine what might happen if you sent a 30-Kbyte file to five people, and each file was stored separately. The 30-Kbyte file would be stored five times, taking up 150 Kbytes. Further, five replies using the **Message to all** command would result in 25 more messages, taking up 750 Kbytes of space. Since cc:Mail stores attachments once and points to them when referenced in a specific message, cc:Mail users don't have to worry about attachments inadvertently chewing up too much hard disk space.

Once you've specified the type of reply you want to make, a window pops up to let you create your reply. The window functions as if you selected the **Prepare message** command. (For a more detailed description of creating messages, refer to Chapter 15.) In general, you type in the reply using the cc:Mail editor, a text editor that has simple cut-and-paste capabilities.

If you need to enclose another text item or other Macintosh files in the reply, click on the **Enclose** button and select a new text item or file. If you select **Text**, a new text window pops up. If you select **File**, the following menu pops up:

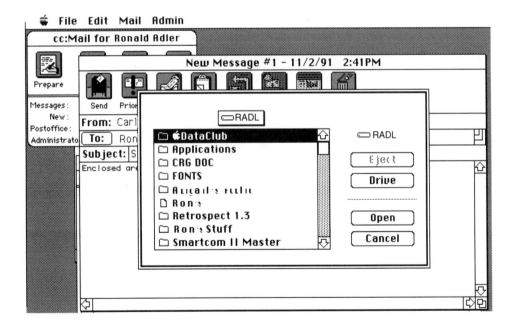

Figure 14-4. The File selection window

Like all Macintosh file-selection menus, you change the folder by holding the menu down and moving backwards up the hierarchical tree of folders until you reach the folder you want to open. When the correct folder is open, click twice on the file you want to enclose. Assuming the the text reply is one item, you may enclose up to 19 files in a single reply.

You can send your completed reply by clicking on the **Send** button. If you want to send the reply return receipt, click on the **Receipt** button. When receipt is selected, you will be notified when the recipients open up the message in their Inbaskets. You can also change the names in the To: field of the message at this point.

Some e-mail systems cannot enclose the original message with a reply. Enclosing the reply is a very useful function, however, if you receive a lot of short messages. You can include the original message as a reminder of the specific message to which you are replying.

Forwarding a Message

Often, after reading a message, you'll want to forward it to someone else. To forward a message, click on the **Forward** button. A submenu pops up with these choices:

Forward as is

Forward with changes

Forward as new

The **Forward as is** command forwards the message exactly as it was sent to you. When this command is selected, your name is placed in the **From** field, while you select the recipient(s) from the directory that pops up (see Chapter 15 for a discussion on how to address messages). **Forward as is** does not allow you to add any comments to the message. When the message is sent, it is labeled "Forwarded as is" with the name of the original sender.

The **Forward with changes** command lets you change the message, then forward the changed message to another person. When you select this command, you are placed in the directory to address the message. Your name is placed in the From: field. You can open text items and make changes to them as you like. You can also open new text items, or delete any existing message items (text or computer files) by selecting the **Clear** (⌘ K) command. When the message is sent, it is labeled "Forwarded with changes" with the name of the original sender.

The **Forward as new** command creates a new message with the same attachments as the original. You can put your own name and subject line on the message. After completing the new message, click on the **To:** button to fill out the name(s) of the recipient(s). The recipient(s) will not see who sent the original message.

Storing Messages

The **Store** button allows you to save a message in a private folder on the cc:Mail server. Folders are structures inside the cc:Mail server that are similar, but not identical, to folders on your Mac desktop. One distinction is that they can be accessed from any computer on the network with cc:Mail, including an IBM PC. When you press down the mouse button on the **Store** button and hold it, a window with a menu of your current folder titles pops up. Drag the pointer to the folder where you want to store your message and release the mouse button.

If you want to save the message on your PC, you must select the **Save as archive** command from the **File** Menu.

Deleting Messages

To delete a message that is open, click on the **Trash** button. You are asked to confirm that you want to delete the message. Click on the **Yes** button to delete the message. A deleted message cannot be recovered, so be careful with this function.

You can also delete messages when you are in the Inbox listing. Select the message and select the **Clear** command from the Edit Menu. Use the Shift key to select and delete multiple messages. Keep in mind that the server is not an unlimited resource. It can run out of disk space, so keep messages stored in the system to a minimum. Typically messages become obsolete rather quickly. It is usually better to store attachments, such as computer files locally rather than on the server. Be sure to delete messages when you no longer need them.

Saving Message Items to your Desktop

You can save cc:Mail message items directly to your hard disk by clicking on the item and selecting the **Save As** command from the **File** Menu. Select **Save As** to name the item and to select the specific disk drive and folder. Click on the Save button to save the file to a specific folder.

Reading Bulletin Board Messages

Messages posted to a bulletin board are read in the same way as you read messages in the Inbox, except you cannot reply to or forward these messages. To read a bulletin board message, click on the BBoard button in the Control Panel. A window displays the bulletin boards. Double-click on a bulletin board, and a window with a list of specific messages pops up. Double-click on the message you want to read. Click on the close button in the upper left-hand corner of the window to close the message.

CHAPTER 15

Creating and Sending Messages

To create a message, click on the **Prepare** button in the cc:Mail window or select the **Prepare message** (⌘M) command from the **Mail** Menu. The following window pops up:

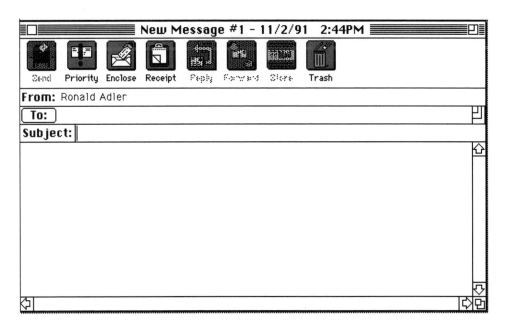

Figure 15-1. Prepare Message window

The window has five active command buttons at the top, along with fields labeled **From:**, **To:**, and **Subject:**. The **From:** field is filled in with the sender's name. The five active buttons are:

- **Send**—sends the message to the cc:Mail server for delivery.

- **Priority**—sets the priority at Normal, Low, or Urgent if a message is to be delivered to a post office via a gateway.

- **Enclose**—allows new text files or computer files to be enclosed within the message as a new item.

- **Receipt**—sends the message return receipt.

- **Trash**—throws away the message.

There are three inactive buttons (**Reply**, **Forward**, and **Store**) that are for reading mail—not creating and sending mail.

Creating a Message

Creating and sending messages requires three basic steps:

- Addressing the envelope

- Creating the message items

- Sending the message

The envelope consists of the **From:**, **To:**, and **Subject:** fields. While the **From:** field is filled in by cc:Mail, you select names from a directory to fill in the **To:** field, and you also enter the subject if one is to appear with the message.

cc:Mail recognizes four types of message items: text (t), graphics (g), computer files (f), and fax files (x). Up to 20 different message items can be created in a single message.

Addressing the Message

Using the directory

To address the message, click on the **To:** field, or select the **Address To** (⌘ **T**) command from the **Mail** Menu. A directory pops up displaying a list of available users on the post office:

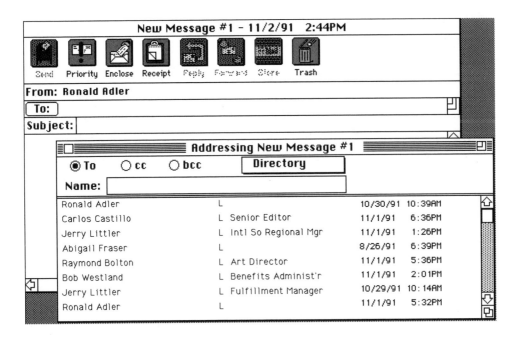

Figure 15-2. Directory of available users

The directory listing contains the name of the user, or the name of a cc:Mail post office that exchanges mail with your local post office, the designation of the user's directory status, the user's title, and the date and time the user or post office last exchanged messages with your post office.

The various status codes are:

- **L** (Local) is a local user on the cc:Mail post office.

- **R** (Remote) is a user who exchanges mail with the post office from a PC via modem.

217

- **r** (remote) is a person who exchanges mail with your post office via another cc:Mail post office.

- **P** (Post Office) is a post office that exchanges mail directly with your post office.

- **p** (post office) is a post office that exchanges mail with your post office via another post office.

- **a** (alias) is another name for a user listed elsewhere in the directory.

Messages to individuals are sent to their mailboxes as soon as the network delivers its messages. Local messages are delivered immediately to the recipient's mailbox. If the recipient's cc:Mail Notify program is running, he or she will be notified automatically. Remote messages are delivered on a set schedule, such as hourly or daily. The delivery schedule is set by your cc:Mail administrator. Most systems communicate once or twice daily. To find out how often your messages are delivered, consult your cc:Mail administrator.

To find a name in the directory, use the up and down arrows in the scroll bar, or type the first few letters of the name in the Search bar at the top of the window. To add a name to your **To**: list, double-click on it, or click on it and press **RETURN**. The name appears in bold in the directory listing and is placed in the **To**: field. Double-click on a name to delete it.

Shift-click to select groups of names. The selected names will appear in bold, while the last name you select will appear in the **To**: field. To see all of the selected names, click on the zoom box at the right end of the **To**: field. If there is more than one recipient, the zoom box will be shaded in black. If there is only one recipient, the zoom box will be white.

Addressing copies and blind copies

In the old days of paper memos, the sender often used the abbreviation "cc" to denote people who received carbon copies. While e-mail does not send literal carbon copies, the abbreviation is still used. Many systems, furthermore, allow blind carbon copies. While a cc is listed on the memo, a bcc is not listed, meaning that other recipients do not know that the copy has been sent to the blind-copy addressee(s).

The "radio buttons" marked **To, cc** and **bcc** determine how each recipient is classified. To send copies or blind copies, click on the copy (**cc**) or blind copy (**bcc**) buttons and then select recipients just as if you were selecting them for the **To:** field. To select a name, double-click on the name, or click on it and press **RETURN**. To select a group of names, shift-click and press **RETURN**. Click on the zoom box in the address field to see the list of bcc recipients.

Sending to a mailing list

You can also use the directory window to address your message to mailing lists, bulletin boards, or folders. The window defaults to the cc:Mail user directory. Click on the pop-up Directory Menu to see the following options:

Directory

Mailing lists

Bulletin boards

Mail folders

Select **Mailing lists**. The **Directory** button changes to say **Mailing lists**, and a list of available mailing lists appears in the cc:Mail window. Double-click on the list to select it, or click on it and press **RETURN**. Shift-click and press **RETURN** to select multiple lists. You will not be able to send blind copies to a mailing list in this fashion, although you can address a list in the **To**: or **cc** fields. When you first log on to cc:Mail, there will be public lists created by your administrator in this directory. To create your own mailing lists, see the section "Creating Your Own Mailing Lists" at the end of this chapter.

Sending to bulletin boards

Bulletin boards are folders containing messages that are available to all users. Bulletin boards are created by your cc:Mail administrator and deal with specific subject areas.

To address a message to a bulletin board, select **Bulletin Boards** from the **Directory** pop-up menu at the top of the address window. A list of bulletin boards appears in the window. (Note that in this window only the **To**: field is available.) All bulletin boards are listed in the **To**: field and are preceded by a pound (#) sign when listed as an address.

Double-click on a bulletin board to select it, or click on it and press **RETURN**. Shift-click to select groups of bulletin boards.

Sending to mail folders

If you want to save a message to one of your mail folders, you can send the message directly to a folder rather than sending the message to your Inbox and then saving it to your mail folder. To save a message to a mail folder, click on the **Directory** button and then select Mail folder.

To select a folder from the list of folders, double-click on the folder, or click on the folder and press **RETURN**. Note that folders in cc:Mail are not hierarchical as they are in other Macintosh applications; in cc:Mail, you cannot nest folders within folders.

Creating a Message

Entering the subject

Once you've addressed the envelope with names from the directory, mailing lists, bulletin boards, or folders, you are placed in the Subject: field. Type in the subject and press **RETURN**. You are then placed in the editor to create your first text item.

Creating text items

cc:Mail offers a simple Macintosh text editor for creating text items. Its purpose is to allow you to type in text, so that the recipient(s) can see a message. cc:Mail does not provide the formatting control that a regular Macintosh word processing program offers. If you want to format your message, create your message in your regular word processing program and send it as an attachment. Remember: the recipient(s) must have the same word processing program in order to read the attachment.

The cc:Mail editor wraps text at the end of a line and uses the six main Macintosh editing commands: **Undo (⌘ Z), Cut (⌘ X), Copy (⌘ C), Paste (⌘ V), Clear (⌘ K)**, and **Select All (⌘ A)**. You can select text with the mouse by clicking and dragging, shift-clicking, and double-clicking, just as you would in any Macintosh application.

The **Undo** command undoes your last command. If you make a mistake, such as cutting an object you want to keep, select the **Undo** command. The **Cut** command deletes the selected information from the screen and places it in the clipboard, which is a temporary storage area. The **Copy** command places a copy of the selected information in the clipboard; the selected information in the original document is unchanged. When you select the cut or copy commands, the information you cut or copy replaces whatever is currently in the clipboard. If you want to store something permanently (so it can be inserted in a program) use the Scrapbook desktop accessory that comes with your system software. The **Clear** command deletes the selected information; it works just like the Backspace key. Use the **Clear** command if you have something in the clipboard you do not want to overwrite.

After you have placed selected information in the clipboard using the **Cut** or **Copy** commands, you can insert the information into the message by placing the cursor at the insertion point and selecting the **Paste** command.

When you are finished, click on the **Close** button.

Sending Return Receipts

When you want to know whether a recipient has opened your message, you can click on the **Receipt** button before sending the message. (A check will appear on the button when it is selected.) cc:Mail will notify you when the message is opened by the recipient. Click on the **Receipt** button to deselect it.

Selecting Message Priority

If you are sending a message to a recipient at a different post office, you can choose the priority level. To select a priority, click on the **Priority** button. A menu pops up with three priorities:

√ Normal

Low

Urgent

Normal is automatically selected. To change the priority, select **Low** or **Urgent**. (A check will appear on the button when it is selected.) Most messages should be sent with normal priority.

On some systems, selecting **Urgent** priority will send a message to a remote system faster than the normal delivery schedule. cc:Mail does not always send messages to remote systems right after they are received by the local post office. Many post offices must make long distance calls to other post offices; it would be very expensive if cc:Mail placed a long distance call every time a message was received at the post office. Generally, a cc:Mail post office makes calls at set intervals, such as every one or two hours. In some cases, sending a message as

Urgent overrides the normal delivery schedule and causes the message to be sent almost immediately.

Enclosing Files

A single message in cc:Mail may contain up to 20 separate items. An item is a block of text created in cc:Mail's editor, a Macintosh program, or a data file. If you want your message to have more than one item, click on the **Enclose** button. A menu pops up allowing you to choose **Text** to enclose an ASCII text file that you create in cc:Mail or **File** to enclose any other file on your computer.

Enclosing Text Files

If you select the **Text** command, cc:Mail will open a new window in the cc:Mail editor. Enter the new message as you normally would and click on the close button in the top left-hand corner of the window, or select the **Close** command from the File Menu. The second window will close and you will be back in the New Message window, where you will see the following two text icons, listed as Untitled 1 and Untitled 2:

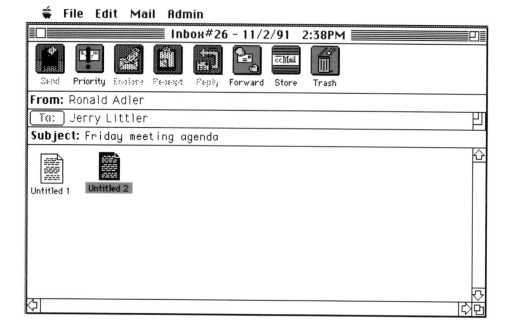

Figure 15-3. New message window with untitled text files

You can move these icons or change their names just as you would any icon on your Macintosh desktop. If you have a large number of enclosures, you can organize them to make it easier for your recipients.

Enclosing other Macintosh files

If you select the **File** command, you will see a dialog box with a list of folders and files from your current disk drive. The dialog box looks like this:

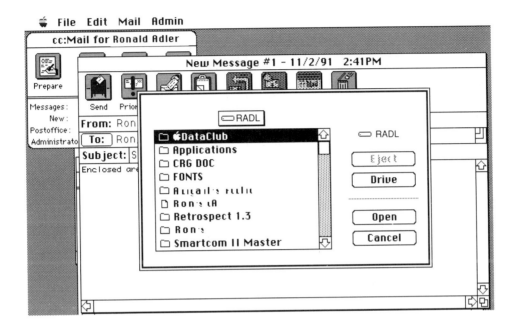

Figure 15-4. Dialog box with the File command

Use this dialog box as you would any Macintosh dialog box. Change the drive, if required, and open folders until you find the file you want to enclose in the message. Select the file and press **RETURN** or click on the **Open** button. The file will appear in the message window as an icon. Although its icon appears in your message window, the original file remains unchanged. A copy is sent with your message when you transmit it.

Sending Messages

When you have finished creating the message, click on the **Send** button. The message will be sent to the cc:Mail post office for delivery. Before sending the message, you must determine whether you want to send it return receipt; you must also select a priority if you are sending to a recipient on another post office and do not want normal delivery.

The Message Log Folder

If you close a message window before you send the message, cc:Mail will ask you if you want to save a copy in your Message Log. This is a folder that you can access later to edit your message before sending it. You can also send it to a folder, instead of to the addressee. (However, make sure that the folder is the only name in the address field.)

Every message you send will be listed in your Message Log folder, so you can refer back to your messages.

Creating Your Own Mailing Lists

A mailing list is a group of names combined together under a single heading, such as all of the people in a single department. When a message is sent to a list, it is sent to everyone on the list.

cc:Mail has two types of mailing lists—public and private. Public lists are created by the cc:Mail administrator, and you create private lists yourself. Version 1.06 of cc:Mail for the Macintosh does not allow you to create private lists. As a result, if you are using cc:Mail Version 1.06 you must use an IBM PC or compatible to create private lists. If you are a Macintosh user with access to a cc:Mail package for an IBM PC or compatible, you can create private mailing lists that you can access later from the Macintosh. (User IDs are independent of computer platform.)

If you have Version 1.1.5, you can create lists with the **Mailing List** command in the **Admin** Menu. A window pops us that lists all of the available mailing lists:

Name	Members
ACCOUNTING	7
BOOKS DEPT.	7
MIS	3
SALES TASK FORCE	10
* ALL USA STAFF	126
* FRONT DESK	7
* MAC USERS	25
* NEWSLETTER TASKFORCE	10
* REMOTE USERS	18

Figure 15-5. Available mailing lists

In the **File** Menu, select **New Mailing List** to create a private list. Your new mailing list will appear in the window with an icon and the name "New Mailing List 1." To open the list, double-click on the icon, or select the list and choose the **Open Mailing List** command from the **File** Menu. A new window pops up with a list of directory names in the right column titled Directory, and a blank left column titled New Mailing List 1.

Selecting names for your mailing list is similar to addressing a message. To select a name for the mailing list, double-click on the name in the directory or click once and press **RETURN**. You can also type the first few letters of the name in the Search bar at the top of the window, which highlights the directory name with the closest match, or calls up names beginning with similar initial letters. This is a quick way to move about the directory.

You can edit your mailing list once it is created. Move to the mailing list column by pressing **TAB** or clicking on the mailing list. To remove an address, either double-click on the name in the list, or click once and press **RETURN**. You can also type the first few letters of the name in the Search bar at the top of the window, as described above. The **TAB** key acts as a toggle between the Directory and the Mailing List, so pressing it again at this point will move you back to the Directory column.

When you are finished, select **Save** from the **File** Menu or click on the **Close** button. You will be asked if you want to save your file first, and will be prompted to name it.

Editing a mailing list

To edit an existing list, select the **Mailing List** command in the **Admin** Menu and double-click on the list you want to edit. Follow the procedures for adding names from the directory or deleting names from the list. If you want to delete an entire list, select the list and then select the **Clear** command from the **File** Menu.

Error Messages for Macintoshes

If personal computers were perfect . . . .

We all know they're not. As a result, a critical part of any program is how it handles errors when they occur. Many programs deliver esoteric messages that only have meaning to the programmer. We've all had experiences where a program has crashed and it says something like, "Error in module DC03:0B16."

cc:Mail tries to give error messages in English, so that users will understand what the problem is. If you receive an error message while using cc:Mail and cannot resolve it, contact your cc:Mail administrator. The error messages are:

Address buffer full.

You have reached the address limit, which is approximately 200 names (4 Kbytes). To add more addressees to the message, you must send the message more than once.

Address list is full.

You are only allowed 200 addressees in a list. You have already added 200 and are trying to add another one.

Bulletin boards cannot be deleted or moved.

You have tried to delete or move a bulletin board. This can only be done by the cc:Mail administrator.

Bulletin boards cannot be moved to folders.

You have tried to move a bulletin board to a folder. This cannot be done in cc:Mail.

Bulletin boards cannot be moved to other bulletin boards.

You have tried to move a bulletin board to another bulletin board. Bulletin boards cannot be nested inside one another in cc:Mail.

Bulletin boards cannot be moved to your Inbasket.

You have tried to move a bulletin board to your Inbasket. Bulletin boards cannot be placed in your Inbasket.

Can't get memory.

There is not enough memory available in the Macintosh to perform the requested function. If you are in the Finder, this means you must add more memory to perform this function if the situation occurs again. If you are in MultiFinder and have several programs open, try closing one or two of the other programs and then retry the function.

Database file not found.

cc:Mail cannot find one of its database files. The file may be damaged on the disk or it may have been deleted.

Database file already locked.

cc:Mail has tried to lock a database file that is already locked. This error should not occur in normal operations and indicates a potentially serious problem. Contact your cc:Mail administrator.

Database file cannot be accessed.

cc:Mail cannot access the cc:Mail database. This means there is some problem with the disk on the server or with the LAN. It could be as simple as the power being off, if the disk drive is separate from the operating system's drive. It could also indicate a serious problem with the hard drive. Reboot cc:Mail and try to access the database again.

Database file already unlocked.

cc:Mail has tried to unlock a database file that is already unlocked. This error should not occur in normal operations and indicates a potentially serious problem. Contact your cc:Mail administrator.

Database file cannot be locked.

cc:Mail tried to lock a file and has not succeeded. This error should not occur in normal operations and indicates a potentially serious problem. Contact your cc:Mail administrator.

Database file cannot be unlocked.

cc:Mail tried to unlock a file and has not succeeded. This error should not occur in normal operations and indicates a potentially serious problem. Contact your cc:Mail administrator.

Database file not locked.

cc:Mail expected to find a file that was locked, but found it unlocked. This error should not occur in normal operations and indicates a potentially serious problem. Contact your cc:Mail administrator.

Database file too large.

This indicates a possible corruption in the database. This error should not occur in normal operations and indicates a potentially serious problem. Contact your cc:Mail administrator.

Database index out of range.

cc:Mail keeps an index of where all messages are stored and lists its parameters within specific ranges. The database has stored a parameter that is out of its defined range. This error should not occur in normal operations and indicates a potentially serious problem. Contact your cc:Mail administrator.

Error opening file.

An error occurred while cc:Mail tried to open a file. Try the command again. If you cannot open the file, contact your cc:Mail administrator.

Folders cannot be moved to bulletin boards.

cc:Mail does not allow you to move a folder into a bulletin board.

Folders cannot be moved to other folders.

Contrary to normal Macintosh operating procedures, cc:Mail does not allow you to move a folder into another folder. In cc:Mail, you may only store messages within folders.

Folders cannot be moved to your Inbasket.

cc:Mail does not allow you to move a folder into the Inbasket, which only stores incoming messages.

Incompatible database.

cc:Mail separates its database from the LAN program and keeps track of program versions for both. You have a database version that does not work with the LAN program version. To solve the problem, you must upgrade your software properly. Contact your cc:Mail administrator.

Individual items cannot be archived.

You have selected an item and tried to archive it. Only complete messages can be archived, not individual items in the message. If you want to place an individual item in your Macintosh, select the item and use the Save As command.

Insufficient disk space for database file.

The drive containing the cc:Mail database is full. Notify your cc:Mail administrator that more space must be allocated to the database file.

Message buffer full.

You have attempted to retrieve a large number of messages at the same time and the message buffer has filled up. Try retrieving a smaller number of messages.

Message cannot be copied.

A disk error occurred while the message was being copied to a folder at the server. Try the function again. If the problem still exists, contact your cc:Mail administrator.

Message cannot be copied. Out of memory.

Your Macintosh has run out of memory to copy the file. If you are in Finder, you will have to add more memory. If you are in MultiFinder, exit other programs you have running and retry the command.

Messages cannot be moved to your Inbasket.

You have tried to move a message to your Inbasket, which houses only incoming messages.

Message cannot be read.

The message you are trying to access is damaged and cannot be read. Contact your cc:Mail administrator. It may be possible to clear up the problem.

Message cannot be stored.

A disk error occurred while cc:Mail was trying to store your message on the server. Either the temporary storage area housing one of the message items has been damaged or the area on the hard disk allocated for the message is damaged. If the message can be read on your screen, save it to your hard disk temporarily and contact your cc:Mail administrator.

(Name) is not in the Mail Directory.

You have entered a name that is not listed in the directory while trying to access cc:Mail. Try to re-enter your name. You may have made a typing mistake. If that does not work, contact your cc:Mail administrator, who should be able to get you access to your account again.

No existing password.

The password you entered was not valid. Try entering it again. If that does not work, contact your cc:Mail administrator, who should be able to get you access to your account again.

Not enough memory to attach file.

Your Macintosh has run out of memory to attach the file. If you are in Finder, you will have to add more memory to perform this function. If you are in MultiFinder, exit other programs you have running and retry the command.

Only the original author can delete this message.

You have attempted to delete a message that you did not create from a bulletin board.

Only the original author can remove this message.

You have attempted to remove a message that you did not create from a bulletin board.

Page table full.

cc:Mail keeps an internal page table that has become full. This error should not occur in normal operations and indicates a potentially serious problem. Contact your cc:Mail administrator.

Sorry, that password is incorrect.

The password you entered was not correct. Try entering it again. If you cannot get access, contact your cc:Mail administrator. If an error has occurred, your administrator can get you access to your account again.

Unable to add another addressee. Out of memory.

Your Macintosh has run out of memory to enter another address. If you are in Finder, you will have to add more memory to perform this function. If you are in MultiFinder, exit other programs you have running and retry the command.

Unable to attach file, disk is full.

The disk on your cc:Mail server is full. Ask your cc:Mail administrator to free up more disk space.

Unable to change password. Out of memory.

Your Macintosh has run out of memory to change the password. If you are in Finder, you will have to add more memory to perform this function. If you are in MultiFinder, exit other programs you have running and retry the command.

Unable to copy entire address list. Out of memory.

Your Macintosh has run out of memory to copy the entire address list. If you are in Finder, you will have to add more memory to perform this function. If you are in MultiFinder, exit other programs you have running and retry the command.

Unable to delete folder(s). Out of memory.

Your Macintosh has run out of memory to delete the requested folder(s). If you are in Finder, you will have to add more memory to perform this function. If you are in MultiFinder, exit other programs you have running and retry the command.

Unable to delete message(s). Out of memory.

Your Macintosh has run out of memory to delete the requested message(s). If you are in Finder, you will have to add more memory to perform this function. If you are in MultiFinder, exit other programs you have running and retry the command.

Unable to detach message item. Disk is full.

There is not enough disk space on the disk where you want to place a message item so it can be accessed independently from the message. Try another disk or free up more space.

Unable to move message(s). Out of memory.

Your Macintosh has run out of memory to move the requested message(s). If you are in Finder, you will have to add more memory to perform this function. If you are in MultiFinder, exit other programs you have running and retry the command.

Unable to return receipt. Disk is full.

There is not enough disk space on the server to send a message with a return receipt. Contact your cc:Mail administrator to free up more disk space.

Unable to return receipt. Out of memory.

Your Macintosh has run out of memory to send the message with a return receipt. If you are in Finder, you will have to add more memory to perform this function. If you are in MultiFinder, exit other programs you have running and retry the command.

Unable to return receipt. Sender name not in mail directory.

During the course of this session, your name has been damaged or deleted on the server and cc:Mail cannot list you in a return receipt. Your cc:Mail administrator will need to reenter your name properly.

cc:Mail for Windows and Beyond

USING CC: MAIL

cc:Mail Windows

The most recent member of the cc:Mail family is a version of the program that runs under Microsoft Windows 3.0. Windows makes most computer programs fairly intuitive to use, provided that you understand the underlying philosophy of the program in the first place. Be sure to read Chapters 1, 2, and 3, which are overviews of electronic mail and cc:Mail. If you understand e-mail in general, and the underlying philosophy of cc:Mail in particular, you'll find it is very easy to use cc:Mail in the Windows environment. In fact, once you learn the basic icon commands, you can start using cc:Mail right away.

About Windows

This chapter assumes that you know the basics of Windows, including using the mouse, selecting and opening applications, manipulating windows (scrolling, resizing, dragging, etc.), and also that you know how to use the Windows editor. If you are not familiar with Windows, we recommend that you refer to Michael Hearst's *Windows 3.0 By Example* (M&T Books, 1990).

cc:Mail Windows Requirements

To run cc:Mail in a Windows environment, you must have an IBM PC AT or higher (a 386 is strongly recommended), at least 2 megabytes of RAM memory, 2 megabytes of space on your hard disk, an EGA or higher monitor, and a 1.2M 5.25-inch or 1.44M 3.5-inch floppy diskette.

cc:Mail is installed on a server on your LAN. Your workstation will link to your server to retrieve all information associated with e-mail operations.

Installing cc:Mail Windows

You install cc:Mail Windows by running an install program on the diskette provided by your cc:Mail administrator. Put the diskette in the floppy diskette (we assume drive A:) and from your hard disk drive type A:INSTALL. You will be prompted for the directory name and path to install the programs.

When the installation is complete, the cc:Mail icon (which looks like a postage stamp with the word cc:Mail in the center) will be installed in the Applications window of Program Manager as shown:

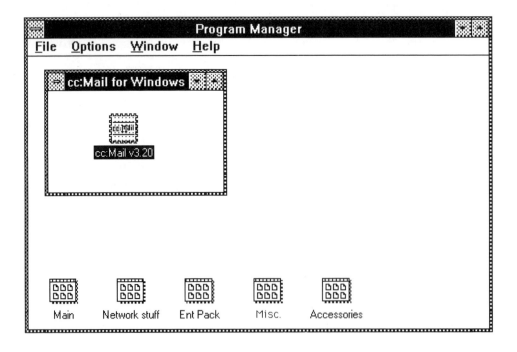

Figure 17-1. The cc:Mail Windows icon

To run cc:Mail, double-click on the icon. The Login window pops up as shown:

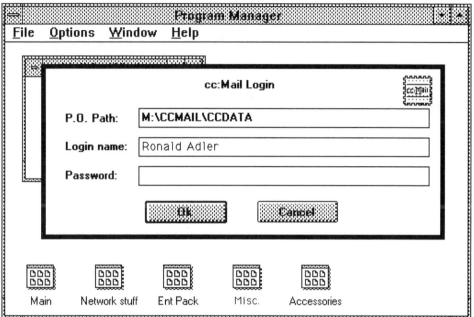

Figure 17-2. The cc:Mail Windows Login window

In regular cc:Mail, you are expected to provide the pathway to the cc:Mail data files in a command line, along with your name and password. In Windows, you type in the pathway, name, and password the first time you run cc:Mail. The pathway and your name are automatically stored, and the next time you log in to cc:Mail, you click on the cc:Mail icon and are only asked for your password.

You can set up cc:Mail Windows so that your password is automatically entered every time you log in. To do this, you must define the cc:Mail section of the WIN.INI file to include the key word PASSWORD= [your password]. However, for security reasons it's a much better idea to have cc:Mail prompt you for your password every time you log in.

When you get into cc:Mail Windows, you see the following Main Menu:

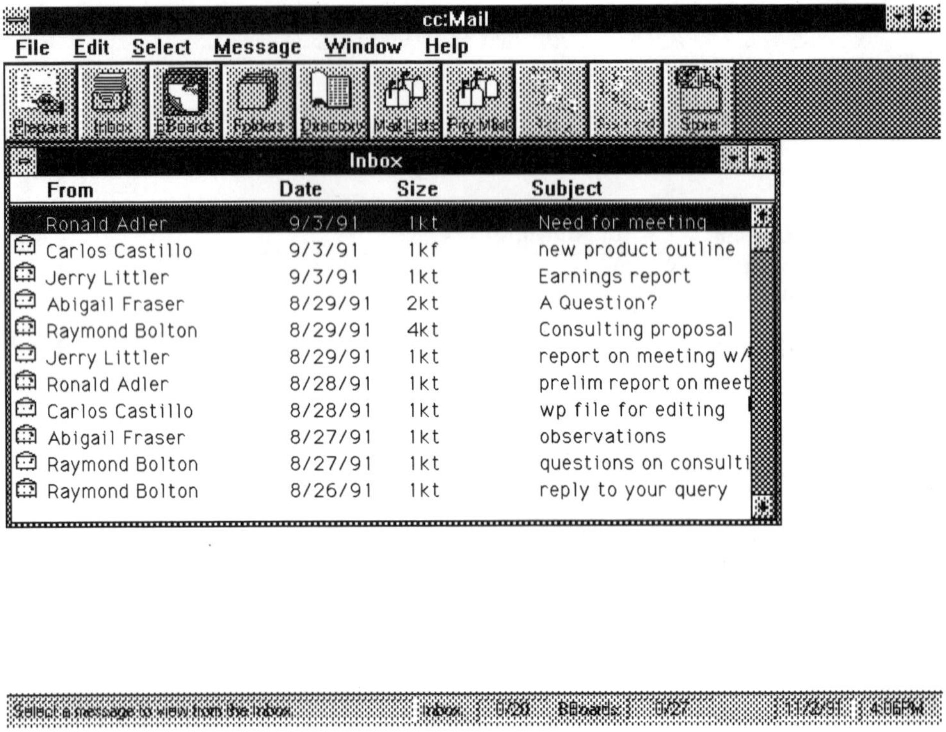

Figure 17-3. The cc:Mail Windows Main Menu

The Windows standard menu is at the top of the screen, with six banks of commands: **File**, **Edit**, **Select**, **Message**, **Window**, and **Help**. Below the menu is a horizontal row of Button commands. You can select the Button commands by clicking on them. Because cc:Mail has such a limited set of commands, you can use the Button commands for more than 90 percent of all cc:Mail operations. The Button commands are:

Prepare

Prepare a new message in cc:Mail.

Inbox

Access your Inbox, which houses all incoming messages until they are deleted or moved.

Bboards

Access bulletin boards, which are open forums for anyone with local access to the cc:Mail post office. When you select this command, you see a list of bulletin boards. When you click on a bulletin board, it displays messages just as if it were an Inbox. Click on a message to read it.

Folders

Access your folders, which are private files in which you can store your messages. While bulletin boards are created by the cc:Mail administrator, folders are created by individual end users, who may create up to 200 folders each, with 200 messages per folder. You can select the Folder command to see a list of folders. Click on a folder to see the messages inside, and click on a message to read it.

Directory

Access the user directory, which is created by your cc:Mail administrator.

Mail Lsts

Access the mail lists that are created by the cc:Mail administrator and available to all LAN users.

Priv Mlists

Access the private mail lists that you have created yourself.

Attach

Attach a text, graphics, or DOS file, or a snapshot to a cc:Mail message. Because of Windows' capabilities, you can also launch another application, create a file, and then go back to the Attach command in sequence.

Send

Send a message.

Reply

Reply to a message you have received.

Forward

Forward a message to another user or users.

Store

Store a message in a folder.

cc:Mail Windows and Regular cc:Mail Compared

The cc:Mail Windows program is a User Agent that has the same basic functionality as the regular cc:Mail user program (for more on User Agents, see Chapter 2). In both programs, you can read and respond to messages, and prepare new messages in the unique ways that cc:Mail has developed. There is a significant difference in how the programs flow, however. Regular cc:Mail cycles you through a series of different menus (shown in Chapter 3), while cc:Mail Windows uses a graphical user interface in which commands are on pull-down menus and/or on the Button commands just below the Main Menu commands.

cc:Mail Windows operates by cycling through the various commands in logical fashion; i.e., when you are in a **Read** cycle, you'll first enter your Inbox and then click on the message you want to read. To write a reply, click on the **Reply** button. To forward the message, click on the **Forward** button. Throughout the process, keep in mind that cc:Mail operates with the underlying metaphor of an Inbox and Outbox memo system combined with a post office. In fact, cc:Mail is so efficient that it doesn't even have an Outbox because there is no need for it. Once you've finished a message, it is sent directly to the post office.

When you are in the Inbox (or a folder or bulletin board), you can reply to, forward, delete, or store each message. When you create messages, you'll start with the **Prepare** button, address the message, use the graphics or text editors (or even another program) attach files, and then send and/or store the message as required.

Menu Commands

While the **File**, **Edit**, **Window** and **Help** commands across cc:Mail's Main menu are standard Windows commands, the **Select** and **Message** Menus are largely associated with cc:Mail-specific operations.

File Menu

The **File** Menu commands are as shown:

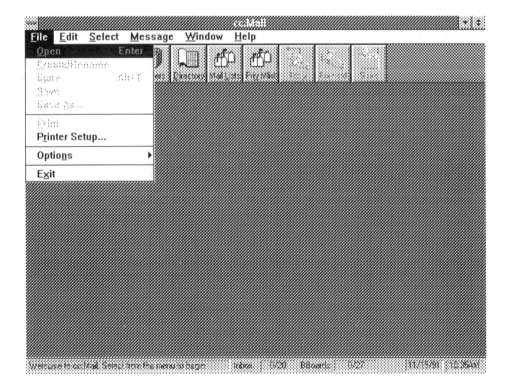

Figure 17-4. The cc:Mail Windows File Menu commands

Open, **Save**, **Print**, and **Printer Setup** are standard Windows commands that are used in association with objects pointed at in cc:Mail. For example, when you select a message, you can open, save, or print it using these commands.

The **Store** command is more specific to cc:Mail and is used to store messages in folders.

The **Options** command opens up a submenu with four choices: **Change Password**, **Display**, **Confirmation**, and **Fonts**. **Change Password**, of course, lets you change your password. If you have been assigned a password by your cc:Mail administrator and have not changed it, you should do so in the first session.

The **Display** command determines the size of the cc:Mail windows, along with what Button commands are displayed. It also determines whether your Inbox opens automatically upon startup. Don't change the Display Options unless you're using a large-screen monitor, you want to control the size of a window, or you don't want to see your Inbox on startup.

The **Confirmation** command asks whether specific types of confirmations should be provided before you complete certain operations the **Undo** command will not reverse (such as deleting messages). In general, it is wise to keep all confirmations active to prevent you from making a mistake that cannot be reversed with the **Undo** command.

The **Fonts** command lets you customize the fonts in your displays. Experiment with this command to find the fonts you like.

The Select Menu

The Select Menu is as shown:

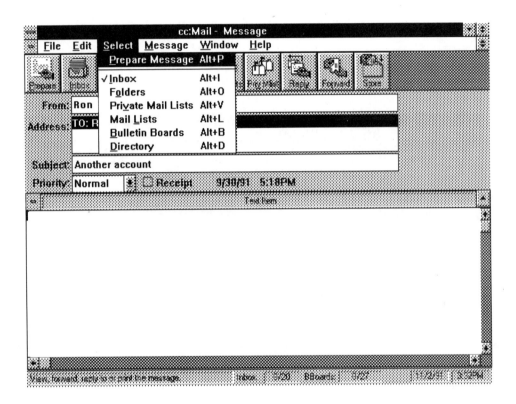

Figure 17-5. The cc:Mail Windows Select Menu

As you can see, the Select Menu duplicates seven of the Button commands: **Prepare Message, Inbox, Folders, Private Mail Lists, Mail Lists, Bulletin Boards**, and **Directory**. These commands are used to access key functions such as preparing a message, reading messages in your Inbox, folders, or on bulletin boards, or viewing the directory or your private mailing lists.

Note: From these basic seven Select Menu commands, you can perform all of cc:Mail's operational functions, except for managing your personal profile. From the Inbox, folders, or bulletin boards, you can read all messages in the system and take appropriate actions. You can create messages with the **Prepare Message** command.

The Message Menu

The Message Menu is as shown:

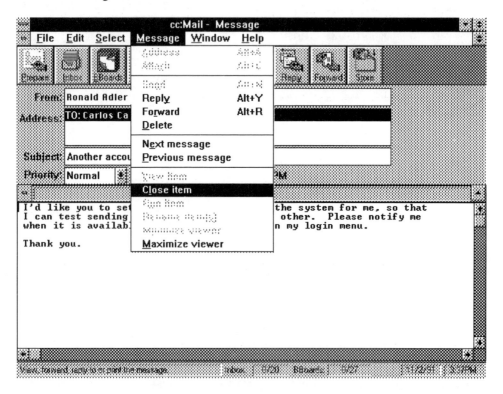

Figure 17-6. The cc:Mail Windows Message Menu

The Message Menu commands operate on specific messages. The **Send**, **Reply**, **Forward**, **Attach**, and **Delete** commands are action commands in which something happens to the message. The **Next message** and **Previous message** commands allow you to select messages. The **View item**, **Close item**, **Run item**, and **Rename item** commands operate on items within a specific message.

The **Run item** command is specific to Windows. It allows the application program associated with the item to be fired up, so that the item can be altered from within its native program. Upon completion, control reverts from the application program back to cc:Mail, and the item remains in the deleted message.

The **Minimize** and **Maximize viewer** commands control the size of the cc:Mail window, so that you can choose between a window sized to fit the full screen or one third of the screen.

Other menus

The Edit, Windows, and Help Menus house editing, Windows control, and cc:Mail **Help** commands. The **Edit** commands are standard Windows **Undo**, **Cut**, **Copy**, **Paste**, and **Delete** commands. The **Search** command allows you to search through folders, bulletin boards, and mailing lists to find messages or names of users/lists.

The Windows Menu allows you to arrange windows and icons on the screen. The **Cascade** command arranges windows on top of each other, with the bottom right edge protruding in each window, while the **Tile** command arranges windows side by side so that every window is visible. The **Arrange Icons** command rearranges icons on the screen in neat rows and columns.

The Help Menu provides cc:Mail help, which is arranged by **Index**, **Keyboard**, **Menu Commands**, **Procedures**, and **Using Help**. If you have any questions while operating cc:Mail, you can often get a fast answer from the Help Menu.

The WIN.INI File

A Windows file called WIN.INI is set up when cc:Mail is initialized. WIN.INI determines a wide variety of cc:Mail parameters. All cc:Mail commands have defaults, but you can change some of these commands by editing the WIN.INI file directly. The commands you can change include:

Password=

If you enter your password, it will be sent to cc:Mail every time you log in so that you do not need to reenter your password every time. While this is convenient, the danger is that anyone who can read the WIN.INI file will know your password. It's always best to keep your password to yourself.

View Style=

Lets you determine how various graphics items will be presented in specific windows. There are three settings: the **0** setting fits the graphic to the size of the viewer window when it was first opened, while maintaining the graphic's aspect ratio; **1** keeps the graphic its actual size, so that it must be scrolled if the graphic is larger than the window; **2** stretches the dimensions of the image to fit the size of the current viewer window.

TextEditor=

Allows cc:Mail to launch an external editor to edit text items when composing a message. To define the specific editor, assign the extension that is assigned to that editor in the Extensions section of WIN.INI. For example, the Windows notepad editor is assigned the .txt extension. To use the notepad editor, add txt after the =, so that the command line reads: **TextEditor=txt**.

GraphicsEditor=

Allows cc:Mail to launch an external editor to edit graphics items when composing a message. To define the specific editor, assign the extension that is assigned to that editor in the Extensions section of WIN.INI.

DefaultWorkPath=

Only use this if instructed by your cc:Mail administrator. It assigns the default work path where cc:Mail's files are contained and is set up automatically when you first log in to cc:Mail.

Notify=

In Windows, you can launch cc:Mail from within the Notify program. If you set **Notify=1**, you will launch cc:Mail for Windows from inside the Notify program. If you set **Notify=0**, you will launch cc:Mail for DOS. Notify will be discussed in more detail later in this chapter.

WrapCol=

Defines the number of columns before text will wrap. The default is 80.

TabStops=

Defines the number of columns moved when the Tab is pressed. The default is 8.

The Notify Program

cc:Mail does not tell you when you have messages. You must check for messages from your PC by either signing on to cc:Mail or running a separate program called Notify. Notify for Windows works almost identically to the DOS version, with a few exceptions. In regular cc:Mail, a window pops up to notify you regardless of the program you are in. You may then leave the program to launch cc:Mail at your discretion. In the most recent versions, cc:Mail's new program, Messenger, makes the Notify program obsolete. Messenger not only notifies you when you have mail, it also lets you pop up a simple User Agent over any program to read the mail, make replies, and prepare new mail.

In cc:Mail for Windows, you do not need the Messenger program because the full cc:Mail User Agent can operate with other applications in Windows' multitasking environment. cc:Mail Windows, however, still needs to notify you if you have new mail, so it has a Notify program. You can choose to be notified by either a pop-up window with buttons or by a flashing icon at the top of the Windows screen. With the Notify window, you can click the OK button to close the window or click on the cc:Mail button to launch cc:Mail directly. You may also have a tone sound to notify you that a new message is available. As in the regular cc:Mail Notify program, you can determine how long between checks—anywhere from 1 to 1,440 minutes.

Note: While you have a lot of options, we suggest that you start out using the Notify Window set for 5 to 15 minutes. That makes it convenient to pop up cc:Mail directly and will prevent you from going for too long with unread messages in your Inbox.

Installing cc:Mail Notify

cc:Mail Notify is a separate program and appears with its own icon and name: WNOTIFY.EXE. To install cc:Mail Notify:

- Make sure your Windows Applications window is active.

- Select **New** from the Program Manager File Menu, so that the New Program Object window opens with the Program Item button active.

- Click **OK** to open the Program Item Properties window.

- Enter the Notify file name and directory in the command line or click the Browse button and select **WNotify** after you find it in its directory.

- If you want the Notify window to appear immediately each time you load cc:Mail, add this line to WIN.INI: LOAD=WNOTIFY.EXE.

Once Notify is set up, there is no need to change it. You will be notified on a regular basis when new messages are received.

Reading mail

When cc:Mail Windows starts up, it automatically opens your Inbox, unless you change the setting using the **Display Options** command. Double-click on a message to read it. The message opens up and then can be acted upon by using the **Reply**, **Forward**, or **Store** buttons.

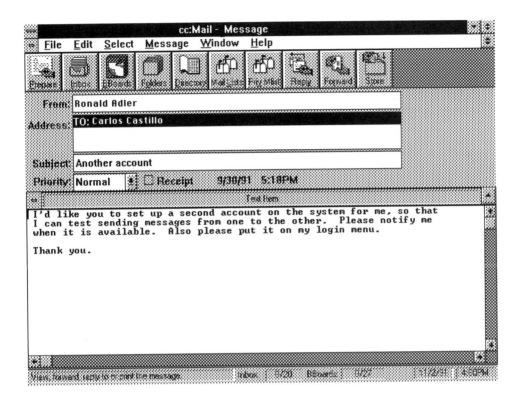

Figure 17-7. A cc:Mail Windows message

One of the few unfortunate oversights of cc:Mail for Windows version 1.0 is that there is no Delete Button command. To delete a message, you must use the **Delete** command from the Message Menu. (A Delete Button is available in version 1.1.)

Note: The reason a Delete button is important is that cc:Mail installations are typically very limited resources that are always looking for more disk space. It is far too easy for users to forget this and store all their messages instead of continually purging unneeded messages. After all, one of e-mail's benefits is that it is paperless. In your own office, if you saved all the paper you received, you'd be flooded. E-mail is neatly stored as blips on a hard disk that, typically, only the mail administrator has to worry about. Remember: if you're using version 1.0 and you do not need a message, *delete it*. If the message is open, use the **Delete** command from the Message

Menu. If you want to delete from the Inbox, select the messages to be deleted and use the **Delete** command from the Edit Menu.

Handling multi-item messages

One of cc:Mail Windows' greatest strengths is the way it handles multiple mail items. A cc:Mail message can have up to 20 items. Each item can be created in one of cc:Mail's editors (text or graphics), or it can be a PC file. This extends across all of cc:Mail's User Agents. cc:Mail for Windows has what are called "viewers" that can display the information created in most popular PC applications, so that when they come in as attachments you can see their contents without having to detach them and run their constituent programs.

When you have a multi-item message in cc:Mail Windows, each item appears with an icon. Double-click on the icon to display its contents. cc:Mail will invoke the correct viewer automatically. You can also launch the application by holding down the **Shift** key and double-clicking on the item.

Viewing Fax Items

If you have cc:Fax, you can view fax items sent to you. cc:Mail saves each fax page as a separate item. When you double-click on a fax page, you may have to move around the page to see all its contents. cc:Mail uses these shortcut keys to help you do this:

Key	Function
1	Sets display scale to a 1/1 ratio (default)
2	Sets display scale to 1/2 ratio
3	Sets display scale to 1/3 ratio
4	Sets display scale to 1/4 ratio
+	Zooms in (max is 1/1 ratio)

-	Zooms out (max is 1/4 ratio)
F	Flips image by rotating it 180 degrees
PgUp	Moves up 1/2 window
PgDn	Moves down 1/2 window
Up Arrow	Moves image up
Down Arrow	Moves image down
Right Arrow	Moves image right
Left Arrow	Moves image left
Home	Moves to top of fax page
End	Moves to end of fax page
Ctrl+PgUp	Moves left 1/2 window
Ctrl+PgDn	Moves right 1/2 window
Ctrl+Home	Moves to left edge of fax page
Ctrl+End	Moves to right edge of fax page

Replying, Forwarding, Storing, and Deleting

cc:Mail for Windows offers the reply, forward, and store functions as button commands. When you select each command, you are given appropriate options; for example, when you select **Reply**, you can check on a box to retain all original addressees or a box to retain all original items in the reply. Since cc:Mail stores message items only once, you do not have to worry about proliferating attached files by shipping them around with replies. If including the original items will help the recipient understand the context of a reply, select the box to retain the original items.

After you have replied to a message or performed a related function, you're still in the message; you can forward, store, or delete it at that point. When you have finished with the message, choose the **Next message** command from the Message Menu to continue with your reading cycle.

Note: In most non-LAN e-mail systems, it is impossible to include the original message in a reply. In cc:Mail, it is almost assumed that you'll include the original. In fact, it is quite common for a cc:Mail user to read a text message, move the editor down below the original message, type in a reply, and then send it back to the originator.

Preparing Messages

To create a message, click on the **Prepare** button. The following window pops up:

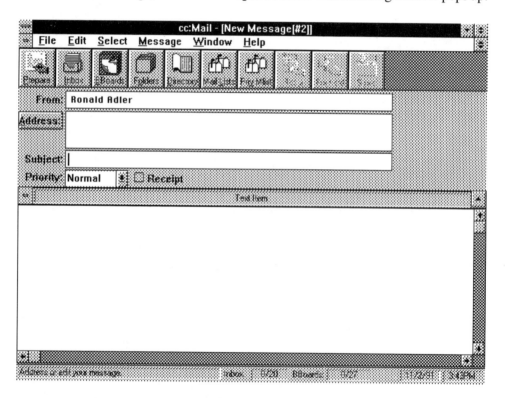

Figure 17-8. An empty Prepare Window screen

To address the message, click on the **A**ddress box below the From: field. Do not click on the Directory button command. The directory pops up:

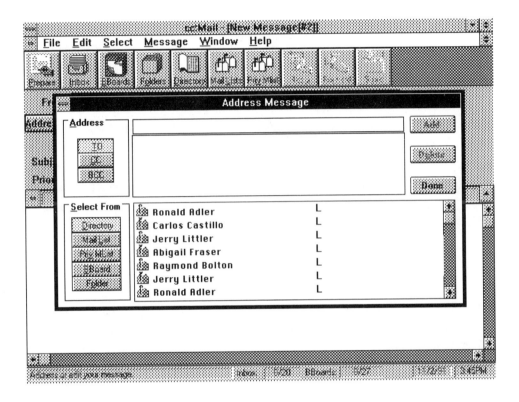

Figure 17-9. The user directory

Select users by clicking on their names. If you see a post office name where a user resides, but not the user's name, click on the post office and then enter the user's name. If you have cc:Fax and want to enter a fax number, click on the generic fax address and enter the fax number in the window that pops up. Directory names are delineated by **L** for local user, **R** for remote user (these users must use the cc:Mail Remote program at your post office. cc:Mail Windows does not yet function as a remote User Agent. You must use the DOS for remote access to a post office), **r** for remote user at another post office, **P** for post office connected directly to your post office, and **p** for post office connected indirectly. When you click on a post office, it opens up and lets you type in the name of the specific user. The name must be typed in correctly or the message will not be delivered.

If you want a mailing list, click on MailList or Priv Mlist in the boxes next to the user directory and you'll get those lists to enter into the **To**: field. If you want to send the message to a folder or bulletin board, click on those boxes as well.

After selecting the addressees and the recipients who get copies (cc) and blind copies (not shown in the **To:** field), you can begin creating the message.

Once you have completed the message, enter the **Subject**: field. Click inside the text editor window to begin creating a text message. If you click the Maximize box, the text editor will fill the entire screen. When you have finished with the text editor, you'll see the file appear as an icon. To attach other files or to create more text items or a graphics item, click on the **Attach** command and select the appropriate vehicle to create a new item. When you have finished attaching items, click on the **Send** button.

Working on Programs from Inside cc:Mail

A simple Attach operation is quite intuitive. Click on the **Attach** button and the Attach window pops up:

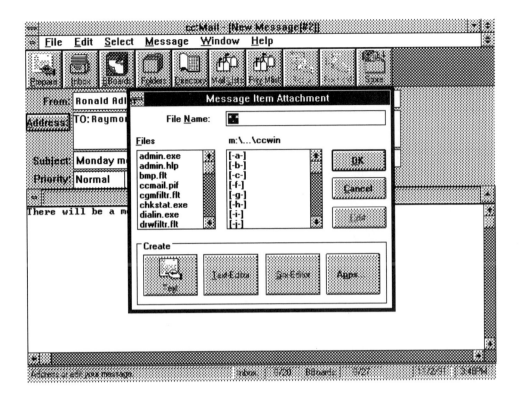

Figure 17-10. The Attach window

Select the file from the appropriate directory. The item will be attached when you press the **OK** button. You can also edit the file by clicking on the **Edit** button command once the item is selected. This will launch the program used to create the original file. After you've finished working on the file, you are returned to cc:Mail. You can then either attach additional files or send the message.

Error Messages

One of the goals of this book is to detail all of cc:Mail's error messages. The following list includes some specific error messages for cc:Mail for Windows.

Refer to the error message list for the DOS User Agent if you receive an error message that is not on this list:

Can't open multiple message items at once.

You have selected more than one message item and tried to open them both. cc:Mail can operate only on one item at a time.

cc:Mail requires ENHANCED or STANDARD mode.

You have tried to run cc:Mail from Windows REAL mode. You must use either ENHANCED or STANDARD mode.

Out of memory.

You have run out of memory. Try closing some windows or other programs.

There is insufficient disk space on your temporary drive.

Your local hard disk is nearly full, preventing you from running cc:Mail. Delete some files to add more space.

Too many logon attempts.

You have tried incorrectly too many times to log on to cc:Mail. Notify your cc:Mail administrator to unlock your account.

Unsuccessful login. Try again?

Press Y and try again. Notify your cc:Mail administrator if you are still unsuccessful at logging on.

You must close open items to delete them from a list.

You tried to delete an item that was open. Close it first.

CHAPTER 18

The Future of cc:Mail

As this book was being prepared, cc:Mail, Inc., the company that developed and publishes the cc:Mail product, was purchased by Lotus Corporation. In addition, Lotus formed a strategic partnership with IBM in which cc:Mail and Lotus' other e-mail product, Notes, are slated to play significant roles. This chapter explores the strategic direction of cc:Mail over the next several years.

The Lotus Acquisition

cc:Mail is no longer a small, independent company in the gigantic sea of software companies. It is owned by one of the leading software companies in the industry. The Lotus purchase is particularly important in light of a long-term technological trend in electronic mail: e-mail is evolving from an isolated, stand-alone program to one that is integrated with application programs and operating systems.

Because Lotus is an industry leader in one of the key software categories, spreadsheets, cc:Mail is now well positioned to become the e-mail platform most closely aligned with the Lotus 1-2-3 family of products.

Integration with Lotus and Other Software Products

One set of steps we should expect from the cc:Mail acquisition are tight integrations with Lotus 1-2-3, Symphony, and the Lotus Notes e-mail products, so that messages can be mailed directly from any of these applications rather than sent from cc:Mail as attachments. This should make it more convenient for a 1-2-3 user to send e-mail via cc:Mail.

cc:Mail's integration with Lotus products will almost certainly lead to further integration with other application programs, so that cc:Mail may become the core e-mail architecture for any application. cc:Mail utility products already allow messages to be submitted directly from application programs; with the Lotus acquisition, these utilities will almost certainly be expanded.

The IBM-Lotus Strategic Alliance

While most strategic alliances have a far weaker impact than expected, IBM's alliance with Lotus may have a very important impact on cc:Mail: direct integration with the OS/2 operating system, enabling OS/2 to provide a mailbox capability to its users.

Summary

cc:Mail is now well established in the field as a stand-alone application; it has a distinct architecture modeled after the operation of a paper-based memo delivery system. In the future, cc:Mail will be coupled with application programs, particularly Lotus 1-2-3 and Symphony, so that messages can be sent directly from within these programs.

In short, cc:Mail will evolve into two separate products. Already, cc:Mail is separated between its "user agents" and its post offices. One post office can handle messages from four different user agents: cc:Mail for PCs, cc:Mail for Macs, cc:Mail for Windows, and cc:Mail Remote. In the future, the post office will open up to direct communications from other application programs, quite possibly even becoming a direct part of the OS/2 operating system.

Appendices

USING CC: MAIL

The Text Editor for PCs

cc:Mail has its own text editor for IBM PCs and compatibles, which cc:Mail calls the Highlighting Word Processor. Don't think of it as a word processing program like Word Perfect, but as an effective and simple editing tool for creating most text messages. And while the text editor is not a word processing program, it has a unique feature for an e-mail editor: cc:Mail's highlight feature lets you emphasize specific points in your message by visually distinguishing blocks of text.

The text editor can store up to 20,000 characters. It operates via **Alt** and function key commands, which means you should keep a list of commands handy if you plan to use the text editor. A short list of commands with their basic functions is shown below. You can also access this list from within the text editor by pressing **F1**:

F1	Displays the help screens
F2	Highlights character at cursor
F3	Moves cursor to last character on a line
F4	Changes margin settings
F5	Marks the beginning of a text block
F6	Marks the end of a text block
F7	Finds a phrase specified in the text
F8	Prints the text or a marked text block
F9	Writes the text or marked block to an ASCII file
F10	Ends the text item
Alt-F1	Changes the highlight settings

Alt-F2	Changes the highlight within a block of text
Alt-F3	Inserts a blank line at current cursor position
Alt-F4	Deletes all characters to end of the line or within block
Alt-F5	Moves a text block to current cursor position
Alt-F6	Copies a text block to current cursor position
Alt-F7	Allows you to replace phrases within text
Alt-F8	Reformats lines within a paragraph or block
Alt-F9	Enters an ASCII file or text snapshot at cursor
Alt-F10	Ends the text item
ENTER	Acts as carriage return to delineate paragraph
Backspace	Deletes the character before the cursor
PgDn	Scrolls the screen down 12 lines
PgUp	Scrolls up 12 lines
Ctrl-PgDn	Scrolls down 24 lines
Ctrl-PgUp	Scrolls up 24 lines
Del	Deletes character at cursor position
Ins	Switches to insert character mode
End	Moves to end of screen
Ctrl-End	Moves to end of text
Home	Moves to upper left of screen
Ctrl-Home	Moves to top of text
Shift-Tab	Moves backward one Tab setting (five spaces)
Tab	Moves forward one Tab setting (five spaces)

Basic Operations

When you begin a new text item, you automatically activate the editor. If you are reading a message and want to use the editor, press any one of the cursor keys, such as the **Up** or **Down** arrow keys, and position the cursor where you want to make changes. The editor will automatically word wrap unless you set the margins at 80 columns. When you are finished typing, press **F10** to return to the appropriate cc:Mail menu, such as the **Send** Menu or **Attach** Menu.

To delete single characters, use the **Del** and **Backspace** keys. Press **Alt-F4** to delete all characters from the cursor to the end of a line, or all characters within a marked block of text—as long as the cursor is within the block. If there are no characters on a line, **Alt-F4** deletes the line itself.

To insert characters, press the **Ins** key to switch from typeover mode to insert mode. The cursor changes from a flat blinking line to a blinking rectangular box. Every character you type will be inserted to the left of the cursor. If word wrap is active, the paragraph will reformat itself automatically. Press **Alt-F3** to insert a blank line at the current cursor position.

As you type, you'll see the following Help bar at the bottom of the screen:

```
L: 11   C: 34   %Full: 1   Highlight (ΔΔΔΔ): AltF1   Help: F1   End: F10
```

Figure A-1. The Help bar while editing

When you are editing, the Help bar shows:

- The line number (L: x)

- The column position on the present line (C: x)

- The percentage fullness in relationship to the 20,000 limit (%Full: x)

- The active Highlight character and key ((ΔΔΔΔ): Alt-F1)

- The Help key (Help: F1)

- The End key (End: F10)

If you are reading a message and have not activated the editor, the Help bar looks like this:

```
Window 1-24   Lines: 45    Edit: ↑↓ ←→    Help: F1    End: ENTER
```

Figure A-2. The Help bar while reading a message

If you have not activated the editor, the Help bar shows:

- The block of lines being viewed (Window: *x-y*)

- The total number of lines (C: *x*)

- The keys to press to edit text (Edit: *arrow keys*)

- The Help key (Help: F1)

- The End key (End: ENTER)

Text Block Operations

The editor lets you mark text blocks: press **F5** to mark the beginning of a text block; press **F6** to mark the end of a text block. Only one block is active at a time; press **F5** to mark the beginning of a new text block.

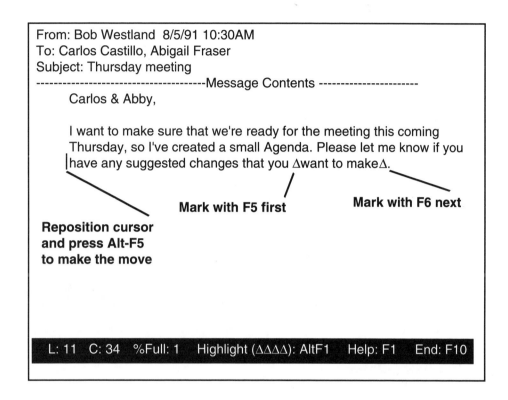

From: Bob Westland 8/5/91 10:30AM
To: Carlos Castillo, Abigail Fraser
Subject: Thursday meeting
---------------------------------------Message Contents ----------------------
    Carlos & Abby,

    I want to make sure that we're ready for the meeting this coming
    Thursday, so I've created a small Agenda. Please let me know if you
    have any suggested changes that you △want to make△.

Mark with F5 first   **Mark with F6 next**

**Reposition cursor
and press Alt-F5
to make the move**

L: 11   C: 34   %Full: 1   Highlight (△△△△): AltF1   Help: F1   End: F10

Figure A-3. Moving a text block

After creating a block, you can delete, copy, move, reformat, or print the text block to paper or an ASCII file. **Alt-F4** deletes the block. **Alt-F5** moves the block to a position just after the cursor so that the text is in a new location. **Alt-F6** copies the block so that the text remains in its original position and a copy is placed in a new position. **Alt-F8** reformats the block to the current left-right margin settings. (If no block is defined, **Alt-F8** will reformat the paragraph where the cursor is located.) **F8** prints the block to paper, and **F9** prints the block to an ASCII file that you specify via a prompt.

Margins and Tabs

cc:Mail lets you set left and right margins at any two of 80 column positions. The default is 11 and 70. The margins operate on a line-by-line basis and can be reset for every line. To change the margin after you've typed in text, use the **F5** and **F6** keys to mark the text, and use the **Alt-F8** key to change the margin.

Press **F4** to set the margins, which appear as follows:

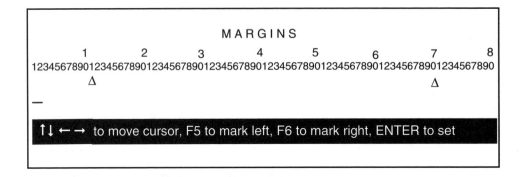

Figure A-4. Margin settings

The cursor is a blinking horizontal line below the first line. Move the cursor to the right and press **F5** for the left margin and **F6** for the right margin. The arrows will change to mark the new position. When you are satisfied with the new margins, press **ENTER**.

Remember: setting the margin at its full 80 columns disables word wrap.

File and Printing Operations

The editor allows you to import ASCII text files and cc:Mail screen snapshots that contain ASCII text and to print either the entire contents or just a block to a printer or to an ASCII file. To import DOS text files, press **Alt-F9** and enter the name of the file, or use the cursor to select the directory and file you want. If you select a directory, the files will be displayed automatically. When you have selected a file, it will be loaded at the cursor position. You will be prompted for the starting and ending lines so you can select the block you want to import. If you do not specify line numbers, cc:Mail assumes you want to import the entire file.

To print, press **F8**; to write to an ASCII file, press **F9**. To print to a file, either type in the drive, directory, and file name you want, or use the cursor to find the directory you want and then type in the name of the file. When you press **ENTER**, the text will be written to the named file.

Highlighting Text

Because the cc:Mail word processing program is primarily used to communicate on PC screens rather than on paper, it has a unique feature that allows you to highlight on-screen text.

Highlighting works on both color and monochrome screens. cc:Mail also translates between color and monochrome screens, so that a message highlighted on a color screen will be displayed appropriately on a monochrome screen and vice versa. On monochrome screens, you can choose underline, reverse video, bold, and bold reverse video. On color screens, you can choose colors for the text and the background from 128 color combinations.

cc:Mail allows you to define the type style you are using. On a monochrome screen, you can choose normal, underline, reverse video, bold, bold/underline, and reverse bold. On a color screen, you can choose the background color and text color. Since the background is applied to every character, you can change both attributes. Think of cc:Mail's highlighting capability as a felt tip pen for highlighting parts of your text.

When you first enter the editor, you are given default settings. The monochrome screen's default is normal characters, and the color monitor's default is white text on a blue background. To change the default settings, press **Alt-F1**. On a monochrome screen, a window pops up with six choices:

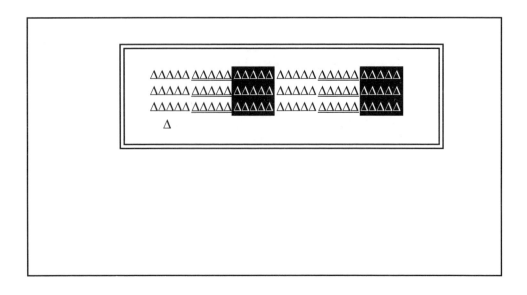

Figure A-5. A monochrome highlight screen

Move the **Left** or **Right** cursor keys to the highlight you want and press **ENTER**. The highlight changes, and the text you enter appears in the selected type style, such as bold.

If you are using a color monitor, a window pops up with 16 foreground (character) colors and 8 background (line) colors. Use the **Up** and **Down** arrow keys to choose the background color and the **Right** and **Left** keys to choose the text color. Press **ENTER** after you've made your choice.

Whether you have a color or monochrome monitor, use **F2** to highlight selected characters.

The Graphics Editor

cc:Mail's graphics editor is unique in the electronic mail world. While such editors have become popular in the Macintosh and Microsoft Windows worlds that operate with a mouse, cc:Mail's editor was developed in the program's early days and was designed for keyboard operation—although it now also works with a mouse.

The cc:Mail graphics editor seems frankly primitive if you have used some drawing programs available for the Macintosh and Windows. Without a mouse, it is also fairly cumbersome to use. While the graphics editor is fine for creating simple drawings, it cannot be used for complex drawings.

The graphics editor works on any IBM PC that has a CGA, EGA, VGA, or Hercules graphics card. Graphics that are created in one mode will be displayed as well as possible in any other mode; i.e., a line drawn with a CGA monitor will be displayed with higher resolution when displayed in VGA mode.

Using the Graphics Program

You get into the graphics editor by selecting "Attach Graphic Item" when you're creating a message or attaching a graphic snapshot. To begin using the program, press **F9** to access the Graphics Menu. The menu looks like an artist's palette, with a variety of icons that represent different drawing tools, as well as several commands.

F9 turns the menu on and off, so that you can draw on a full screen and pop the menu over the bottom and right side portions of the screen.

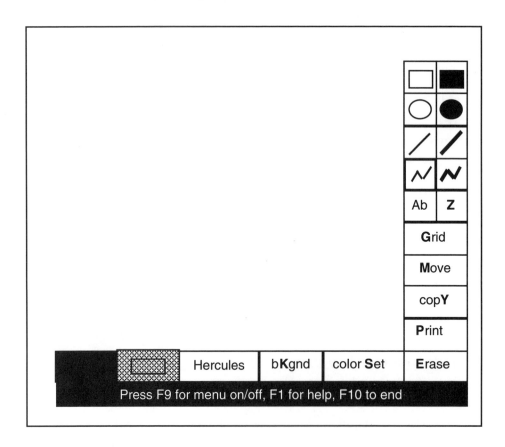

Figure B-1. The cc:Mail Graphics Menu

You select a tool or command by using the **Left** and **Right** and **Up** and **Down** cursor keys and pressing **ENTER**. You are initially located at the thin-line freehand drawing symbol. Keep in mind that the cursor keys are used to move throughout the menu and are also used to draw on the screen after selecting a command. Make sure you know where you are in the program, so you do not press a cursor key to reach a command when it will cause you to draw on the screen—or vice versa.

The **ENTER** and **Esc** keys are also important. When you move to a menu option, **ENTER** executes the command. When using a drawing tool, **ENTER** starts and ends the drawing of lines, boxes, and circles, and also begins and ends move, copy, and erase processes. **Esc** allows you to stop drawing an object if you make a mistake.

Other important command keys are:

- **F1**—the Help key

- **F10**—Ends the drawing and exits the editor.

- **Num Lock** or **Shift**—Changes the drawing resolution of the cursor keys. In regular mode, the cursor keys will draw eight dots at a time. In **Num Lock** or **Shift** mode, the keys will draw one dot at a time.

- **Power Keys**—As in all cc:Mail programs, you can select commands with power-user keys.

Selecting your Resolution Mode

The first thing you must do is set your resolution mode, if it is not set correctly. When you first enter the editor, you are in the Graphics Menu. If you do not like the resolution mode that is displayed, move the cursor to the mode window. It will be highlighted. Press **ENTER**. The mode changes to: CGA Lo-Res, CGA Hi-RES, EGA Lo-Res, EGA Hi-RES, VGA, and Hercules (Hercules Graphics for monochrome monitors). When you are at the mode you want (your PC must support it, of course), leave the selection on the screen and move the cursor to any other choice you want.

Select your Foreground Color

The color windows to the left of the resolution mode determine your foreground color, which is the color in which you draw lines and boxes. Figure B-1 shows two colors because it is in a monochrome mode. Each color is displayed, depending upon the mode. In CGA mode, you can choose one of four colors; in EGA and VGA mode, you can choose from 16 colors. You can change the color at any time. The color affects only what you are about to draw, not what has already been drawn.

Use the **Left** and **Right** cursor keys to move through the color palette, or press the number keys 1–16 as appropriate to move directly to the color. When you are at the color you want for your drawing, press **ENTER**. Notice that as you move over the colors, the selected one is highlighted with a small rectangle in its center.

Select your Background Color

The "b**K**gnd" command allows you to set the background color, which is displayed at the far left of the color bar with a little rectangle in the center. The default setting is blue. You may choose from up to 16 colors. When you select the "b**K**gnd" command, you are moved to the color palette. Move the rectangle to the background color and press **ENTER**. The screen changes to that color. You can have only one background color at a time.

Defining Four-Color Palettes in Low Resolution

For CGA and EGA low-resolution modes, you can display only four colors at a time on the screen. To make it convenient, you can define two palettes (sets) of different colors in two intensities, for a total of four different palettes. The command to use is "color **S**et." When the command is invoked, press the **ENTER** key to toggle among the different palettes. You can alternate as much as you want among the palettes, but keep in mind that low resolution can display only four colors on the screen at a time.

Drawing Tools

The graphics program gives you eight graphics drawing tools, which are displayed at the top of the menu:

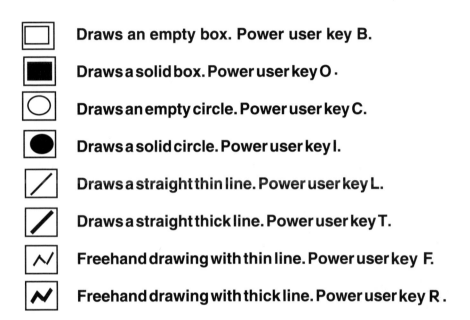

Draws an empty box. Power user key B.

Draws a solid box. Power user key O.

Draws an empty circle. Power user key C.

Draws a solid circle. Power user key I.

Draws a straight thin line. Power user key L.

Draws a straight thick line. Power user key T.

Freehand drawing with thin line. Power user key F.

Freehand drawing with thick line. Power user key R.

Figure B-2. Graphics drawing tools

Text Tools

There are two text tools that allow a graphic to be annotated with text:

Ab allows upper- and lowercase text in an 80 column-x-25 row format.

Z allows uppercase text in 40 column-x-25 row format.

Graphics Commands

There are five graphics commands:

- **G**rid displays a set of regularly spaced dots to help you align objects. To display the dots, move to **Grid** and press **ENTER**, or press the letter **G**; press **G** again to delete the dots.

- **M**ove lets you move a rectangular area of the screen to another part of the screen.

- cop**Y** lets you copy a rectangular area of the screen to another area of the screen.

- **P**rint lets you print the graphics screen.

- **E**rase lets you erase a rectangular area of the screen by setting it to the background color.

Drawing with the Cursor Keys

With the graphics editor, your cursor keys are the primary drawing tools unless you use a mouse. For example, whenever the Right-arrow key is pressed, it will move eight dots to the right on the screen. For greater drawing precision, press the **Shift** key while moving the cursor, or press **Num Lock**. This changes the drawing resolution to one dot per key stroke. You will have to make more key strokes to draw, but you'll be able to fine-tune your drawing within the limits of the program.

Note: Drawing with the cursor keys creates drawings in a temporary color. After you finish the drawing, cc:Mail applies your selected color.

Drawing Boxes

The drawing tools let you draw boxes, either empty or solid. Empty boxes show the background color in the center of the box, with the outside lines in the selected

278

foreground color. In the case of an empty box drawn in black ink on a piece of white paper, for example, the background would be white and the lines would be black. Solid boxes, on the other hand, have the entire foreground color. If the background is blue and the foreground is yellow, a solid box would be yellow.

To draw a box, move the cursor to the empty or color box icon and press **ENTER**, or press the correct power-user key (**B** for empty box and **O** for solid box). Once the command is selected, move the cursor to the place on the screen where you want the top left corner of the box to be drawn and press **ENTER**. Next, move the cursor to the place where you want the bottom right hand corner to be drawn and press **ENTER**. The box will be drawn as you move. You do not have to begin at the top left, but can draw in any direction by moving the cursor keys. As you draw, you can press **Esc** to reset to the original point where you set your cursor, or **F9** to erase what you are drawing and return to the menu.

While this drawing method works, it is cumbersome. Drawing with a mouse is faster and easier than using the cursor keys. Point to the appropriate box icon and press the left mouse button to select it. Point to the screen and press the left mouse key to define the top left corner of the box. Drag the cursor from this corner to draw the box.

Drawing Circles

To draw a circle, move the cursor to either the empty- or solid-circle icon and press **ENTER**, or use the power keys **C** or **I** while in the menu. The empty-circle option will draw the outline in the foreground color and the inside in the background color; the solid-circle option will draw the outline and the inside in the foreground color.

After selecting the type of circle you want, move the cursor to the point where you want the center of the circle and press **ENTER** (you can also move the mouse directly to that point and press the left mouse button). Move the left or right arrow keys horizontally to define the circle's circumference. As you move, you will see lines expand equally in all four directions. When you are finished, press **ENTER**. The circle is drawn and the cursor is moved to the center of the circle, which makes it easier for you to draw concentric circles. As you draw, you can press **Esc** to reset the cursor to its starting point, or **F9** to erase what you are drawing and return to the menu.

Drawing Lines

To draw a line, move the cursor to either the thin- or thick-line icon and press **ENTER**, or use the power keys **L** or **T** while in the menu. Move the cursor to one end of the line and press **ENTER**. As you move the cursor toward the other end point, the line will appear. Use the **Up, Down, Left,** and **Right** cursor keys. If you press two cursor keys at the same time, the line will rotate: pressing the **Up** and **Left** keys simultaneously moves the line left at a downward angle, for example.

When you are finished drawing the line, press **ENTER**. The line will be drawn in the foreground color. As you draw, you can press **Esc** to reset the cursor to its starting point, or **F9** to erase what you are drawing and return to the menu.

Remember: the cursor will move eight dots per stroke unless you press **Shift** or **Num Lock** while pressing the key, which will move the keys one dot at a time.

Freehand Drawing

To draw by freehand, move the cursor to either the thin or thick freehand icon and press **ENTER**, or use the power keys **F** or **R** while in the menu. The **ENTER** key acts as a toggle to either activate or suspend the drawing, so that you can move the cursor to another point and draw a second freehand graphic.

To begin a freehand drawing, move the cursor to the place on the screen where you want to begin and press **ENTER**. As you move the cursor, the line will be drawn. Remember that a temporary color is used when drawing with the cursor. When you are finished, the drawing will revert to the foreground color you have selected. Use combinations of the **Up, Down, Left**, and **Right** cursor keys to move at 45-degree angles. The best way to understand how this works is to experiment.

When you are finished, press **Esc** or **F9**. Note that you cannot use **Esc** to back out of a freehand drawing and erase it. To erase a freehand drawing, you must change the drawing color to that of the background and redraw over the freehand drawing, which will act as an eraser. You may also use the **Erase** command, which will clear a specific area of the screen.

Creating Text

To write on the screen, select either the **Ab** or the **Z** icon and press **ENTER**. Move the cursor to the screen and press **ENTER**. Begin typing. The text will appear.

The **Ab** icon lets you type 80 columns in upper- and lowercase text, while the **Z** icon lets you type in 40 columns in uppercase only.

Moving or Copying

You cannot move or copy an object per se. Moves and copies operate on a rectangular portion of the screen in which the object resides. To move or copy an object, select the **M**ove or cop**Y** command in the Graphics Menu. Move the cursor to the top left corner of the area you want to select and press **ENTER**. Move the cursor to the bottom right and press **ENTER**. The selected area will be outlined, and vertical and horizontal guidelines will appear to help you define a proper position to move the selected area.

Move the selected outline by pressing the cursor key that corresponds to the direction in which you want the outline to move or be copied. As you press the cursor key, the object moves along. When you press **ENTER**, the action is completed. If you change your mind and do not want to complete the move or copy, press **Esc** or **F9** to abort the impending move or copy. If you select **Move**, the selected area of the screen is moved and the original area is set to the background color; if you select **Copy**, then you have a duplicate at two screen positions.

Erasing

You can erase any portion of your drawing by selecting an area and having that area set to the background color. Select the **E**rase command from the Graphics Menu. Select the area to be erased by first moving to the top left point and pressing **ENTER** and then moving to the bottom right and pressing **ENTER**. The selected area is shaded. When you press **ENTER** again, the area is erased. If you change your mind after selecting an area but before erasing it, press **Esc** to erase the selected area, leaving the original screen intact. Otherwise, press **F9** to return to the Graphics Menu without making any changes.

Printing

To print the drawing (not the menu, if it covers a corner of the drawing), select the **Print** command from the Graphics Menu. The image will be printed using different gray-scale images to represent different colors. (You must, of course, have a printer that can print graphics.)

Using the Grid

At any point while drawing, selecting the **G**rid command puts up columns and rows of dots to help you align objects you are drawing. To turn the grid off, select the command again. You select the command by moving to the command and pressing **ENTER** or by pressing the **G** key while in the Graphics Menu.

Leaving the Editor

When you are finished with your drawing, press **F10**. You are returned to the place in cc:Mail where you entered the editor, and the drawing is created as a graphics item within a cc:Mail message. If you have the grid turned on when you press **F10**, the grid is automatically removed.

Benefits of the Graphics Editor

When the cc:Mail graphics editor was first created, it was a rarity. Today, it is a primitive screen-drawing program compared to any of the drawing programs available for either PCs or Macintosh computers.

The graphics editor does have a few positive points, however. First, if you plan to send a fax to someone and you have cc:Fax, anything drawn in the editor will be sent automatically. In comparison, you cannot use a PC or Macintosh drawing program and send the result via cc:Fax—at least not directly. The graphics editor also provides you with some interesting options when used in conjunction with the SNAPSHOT.COM program (see Appendix C).

If you want to create a complex graphic, use a drawing program, although you *must* keep your drawing to a single screen. To send the drawing as a fax or to send it to any cc:Mail user, copy the graphic using a snapshot. Snapshots are saved as graphics items, which can be edited in the cc:Mail graphics editor, sent to all cc:Mail users, or sent as a fax to any fax machine in the world if you have the cc:Fax option.

Screen Snapshots

cc:Mail's SNAPSHOT.COM is a unique program that allows you to take screen "snapshots" while you are in any application program, including cc:Mail itself. A screen snapshot is just what it sounds like—a picture of a specific screen in a program. A snapshot can be a few rows and columns in a spreadsheet, a table in a word processing program, a graph or chart from a business graphics program, or anything that can be displayed on a screen.

When you take the snapshot, you save it as a file in any directory you choose. You can then attach the snapshot to a cc:Mail message or edit the snapshot, using the text editor for text or the graphics editor for graphics.

SNAPSHOT.COM is a separate program not integrated into cc:Mail and can be used for any purpose. Any time this program is running, you can take snapshots and store or print them (using the **Print Screen** key).

Running the Program

To load SNAPSHOT.COM, move to the directory where it is stored and type **SNAPSHOT** if you have a color monitor, or **SNAPSHOT MONO** if you have a monochrome monitor. If the directory is part of a startup path statement, you can start SNAPSHOT.COM from any directory. Typing SNAPSHOT runs a TSR (Terminate and Stay Resident) program that takes up 20 Kbytes in your PC's memory. As long as the application program you are running doesn't need that memory, you'll be fine. If you have SNAPSHOT running and strange things happen to an application program, remove the SNAPSHOT program.

You have two choices when you run the program. You can select the key that pops up the SNAPSHOT program, or you may see just a specific file. The default key for SNAPSHOT is **Alt-F1**. You can change the default to **Alt-3** by typing **SNAP-**

SHOT Alt3. If you want to remove the program without rebooting your PC, type **SNAPSHOT REMOVE**. If you just want to see one snapshot file, type **SNAPSHOT @[filename]**; for example, **SNAPSHOT @BARCHART**. The snapshot will be displayed and the program removed.

Taking Snapshots

True to its name, SNAPSHOT is a snap to use. Let's say you use the default **Alt-F1** key. Any time you want to take a screen snapshot of text, press **Alt-F1**. A menu pops up with two choices:

Figure C-1. The Snapshot Menu

If you want to take a snapshot, press **ENTER**. You are prompted to type the directory and file name for the snapshot:

```
═══════════════ cc:Mail SNAPSHOT ═══════════════
    Take snapshot and store in file C: __

Type the filename and press ENTER, F1 for directory,  Esc to cancel
```

Figure C-2. Prompt when taking a snapshot

If you type a file name that already exists, you are asked if you want to replace that file with the new snapshot. If you answer **N** for No, you are asked to give a new file name to your snapshot; the snapshot will be stored by the new file name.

There is no menu for taking a snapshot of a graphics file. The snapshot is taken and stored in your current directory with the first four letters (SNAP), the type of graphics used, and a unique number in the DOS extender. If you are using a Hercules monitor and it is the first graphics snapshot taken in that directory, the file name will be SNAPHGC.001. Up to 999 graphics snapshots can be stored at a time in any single directory.

Displaying Snapshots

If you want to display a snapshot, press **Alt-F1** (or your selected key) and select the "**D**isplay stored snapshot" command from the Snapshot Menu:

Figure C-3. Displaying a snapshot in the Main Menu

After selecting the "**D**isplay stored snapshot" command, you are prompted to type in the directory and file name:

Figure C-4. The display snapshot prompt

You must enter a drive and directory, but if you do not know the file name, press **F1**. A list of files pops up, so you can type in the name of the file you want and press **ENTER**.

When you type in the file name, the screen changes to the selected snapshot. You can view it or print it (use the **Print Screen** key on your keyboard). When you are finished, press any key to return you to where you started.

Annotating or Editing Snapshots

You can edit a text snapshot or annotate a graphics snapshot using cc:Mail's text and graphics editors. For more on using these editors, refer to Appendices A and B, respectively.

cc:Mail Commands

This appendix lists and explains all of the cc:Mail menu commands.

Action Menu

Pops up after reading a new or old message and after displaying the items in a message being prepared. Follows the "**R**ead inbox messages" command in the Main Menu after reviewing a message; the "Act on messages" command in the Retrieve Menu after selecting messages to be retrieved; and the "display **M**essage" command in the Send Menu while looking at items that have been created.

Commands

Address message—This shortcut lets you reenter the directory to add new addresses after displaying items in a message being prepared.

archi**V**e message—A storage option used after reading a message.

attach new i**T**ems—Used to add new items while a message is being prepared.

c**H**oose another item—Used to review another item in a message being prepared or when reading messages in your folders or bulletin boards.

Copy to folder—Used when reading new or old messages, or messages you are preparing.

c**O**py item to dos file—Used solely when reading a message with DOS files attached. Allows the item(s) to be detached back to your PC.

Delete message(s)—Deletes the message(s) being read, whether new or previously read.

display **A**ll items—Walks you through the items in a message in sequence. You can take action on each item as it appears.

display **A**ll messages—Walks you through all the items in all the messages selected in sequence. You can take action on each item in every message as it appears.

display file **I**tems—Available only when DOS file items are attached. Displays as much as it can of these items and allows actions such as detaching the item back to your PC.

display **I**tem—Displays the selected item.

display **N**ext message—Displays the next message in the list that has been selected.

edit s**U**bject—Edits the Subject: field. Available only when displaying items while preparing a message.

Erase item—Eliminates an item being displayed from the message. Used while reviewing items that have been attached to a message you are preparing, or to a message you have stored in your folders.

Forward message—Used to forward a message to other people, typically with your comments attached.

List item titles—Used when reviewing a message to list and edit the titles of all items attached to the message.

Move to folder—Takes the message you have read from the folder it is in and moves it to another folder. Typically used to transfer a message from the Inbox to a named folder for storage.

Print message(s)—Prints the message you have read to a printer.

repl**Y** to message—Allows you to send a reply to a message you have read.

Return to main menu—Allows you to jump directly to the Main Menu and ends actions being performed on the messages.

Send message—Sends the message to the addressees in the To:, cc:, or bcc: fields.

Write to ascii file—Allows you to store a copy of the message in an ASCII file. If the file is the name of a serial port, it will allow you to send the message to a printer other than the one that is the default printer.

Address Menu

Pops up after you have chosen to reply to a message or prepare a new message. Allows you to fill in the **To:**, **cc:**, and **bcc:** fields of the message.

Commands

Address to person—Pops up the cc:Mail directory to select addressees for the **To**: field.

address to bboard/**F**older—Pops up a list of bulletin boards and folders to select as addressees. Used to store a copy of the message; it is particularly valuable when you want to temporarily store a message in progress or store copies of important messages.

address to **M**ailing list—Pops up the list of mailing lists that are available to you. A mailing list has multiple addressees and allows a message to be sent to multiple people using one command.

Blind copy to person—Pops up the mailing list to select people who will receive copies of the message, but whose names will not be visible to other recipients.

cancel receipt re**Q**uest—Cancels the receipt-request command.

copy to mailing **L**ist—Pops up the mailing list to send a copy of the message to a list. A copy is identical to a regular address in cc:Mail; the names will appear in the **cc**: field.

copy to **P**erson—Pops up the directory to select people who will receive copies of the message; the names will appear in the **cc**: field.

Delete address list—Eliminates the entire address list, so that new addresses can be entered.

e**N**d addressing—Completes the addressing sequence and returns you to the Send Menu if you are sending or replying to a message, or to the **Subject**: field if you have just addressed a new message.

Return to main menu—Allows you to jump directly to the Main Menu; you will lose the message if it has not been stored. You will be prompted for verification.

re**Q**uest receipt—Notifies you when a recipient has read your message. Only users in the **To**: field will return receipts.

Attach Menu

Pops up after you have created at least one text item and want to attach more items. It follows the Send Menu when selecting an "attach new i**T**ems command." The menu lists the various types of items that can be attached.

Commands

attach bboard/folder **M**essage—Allows you to attach the items from a message stored in a bulletin board or folder. All items are displayed in sequence so they can be edited if appropriate. At any point, you can cancel the command by pressing **Esc**.

attach copy of dos **F**ile—Allows you to attach DOS files to the message being prepared.

attach **G**raphics item—Allows you to attach a graphics item to the message being prepared. When invoked, you enter the cc:Mail graphics editor. See Appendix B for more details.

attach **S**napshots—Allows you to attach snapshots of screens taken with the cc:Mail Snapshot program and stored in your PC. See Appendix C for more details.

attach **T**ext item—Allows you to add a new text item to cc:Mail. When invoked, you are placed in the editor to create a new text item. See Appendix A for more details.

e**N**d attaching—Ends the attaching sequence and takes you back to the Send Menu.

Folder Menu

Pops up a list of commands that allow you to manage your folders. Pops up after selecting the "manage **F**olders" command from the Manage Menu.

Commands

add **N**ew title or select another—Allows you to add a new folder or to select an existing folder.

Change folder title—Allows you to change the name of a selected folder.

Delete folder—Allows you to delete a folder and all the messages stored within it. Each message will be eliminated from cc:Mail unless it is saved in another folder or by another user. You will be prompted for verification.

Return to main menu—Allows you to jump directly to the Main Menu and ends actions being performed on the message.

Mailing List Menu

Pops up when you select the "manage **M**ailing list" command from the Manage Menu.

Commands

Add names to mailing list—Pops up the cc:Mail directory so you can add new names to a mailing list.

add **N**ew title or select another—Creates a new mailing list or selects another list for maintenance.

Change mailing list title—Allows you to change the name of a mailing list.

Delete mailing list—Deletes the selected mailing list. The names are not deleted from the cc:Mail directory.

Erase names from mailing list—Allows you to select and erase individual names from the mailing list.

Return to main menu—Allows you to jump directly to the Main Menu and ends actions being performed on the message.

View mailing list—Allows you to see the members of a mailing list.

Main Menu

The first menu shown when you enter cc:Mail, this has five main commands:

Commands

e**X**it—Leave cc:Mail.

Prepare new message—Allows you to create a new message. Creates a screen for the new message and displays the Address Menu.

Read Inbox messages—Allows you to read messages in your Inbox. Pops up a list of messages in the Inbox to be selected for reading.

re**T**rieve message—Allows you to look at messages stored in your bulletin boards and folders. Pops up the Retrieve Menu.

Manage mailbox—Allows you to perform management actions on your mailing lists, folders, and password. Pops up the Manage Menu.

Manage Menu

Allows you to perform management tasks on your folders, mailing lists, and password. Pops up after selecting the "Manage mailbox" command from the Main Menu.

Commands

Change profile—Allows you to change your cc:Mail password, printer port, and printer type.

manage Folders—Allows you to add, delete, and change the name of your folders. Takes you to the Folder Menu.

manage Mailing lists—Allows you to add, delete, and change the name of your mailing lists. Takes you to the Mailing List Menu.

Return to main menu—Allows you to jump directly to the Main Menu and ends the actions being performed.

View mail directory—Lets you view the mail directory.

Profile Menu

Allows you to change your password and printer configurations.

Commands

Change password—Allows you to change your password.

change Printer port—Allows you to select LPT1, LPT2, or LPT3 as your printer. If you use a serial printer, use the DOS command COMx = LPTx to reroute the printer. The default is LPT1.

change printer Type—Allows you to switch between text only, graphics, and HP LaserJet printers in standard and fine modes. The default is text only.

Return to main menu—Jumps you directly to the Main Menu.

Retrieve Menu

Allows you to read messages stored on public bulletin boards and in your folders. Pops up after selecting the "reTrieve messages" command from the Main Menu.

Commands

Act on messages—Allows you to take action on messages after you have retrieved them. Pops up the Action Menu.

reselect all Messages—Allows you to recontinue the selection process. It is available after you have already retrieved messages and are back in the Retrieve Menu.

retrieve from archiVe file—Allows you to search your archived messages to retrieve specific messages.

retrieve from bboard/Folder—Allows you to search your bulletin boards and folders to retrieve specific messages.

retrieve from Inbox—Allows you to search your Inbox to retrieve specific messages.

Return to main menu—Allows you to jump directly to the Main Menu and ends the actions being performed.

scan message Headings—Lets you see the headings of all messages stored in cc:Mail. You can move through the list and select messages to be retrieved.

search by Calendar date—Allows you to search for all messages within specified dates. Use the form mm/dd/yy to specify the dates.

search by Keyword phrase—Allows you to retrieve all messages with a specific phrase (of up to 30 characters) in either the Subject: field or item title fields of the message.

search by Person—Allows you to retrieve all messages sent by or to a specific person.

search by priority **L**evel—Allows you to retrieve all messages by designated priority level, such as Urgent.

search for msg n**U**mbers—Allows you to retrieve all messages in a specific folder with the designated message numbers.

search for **N**ew messages—Allows you to retrieve all messages that have not yet been read.

Send Menu

Performs tasks associated with preparing a message, including sending the message. Sending is almost always performed from the Send Menu, although a message being reviewed under some circumstances can also be sent from the Action Menu. Pops up after completing all editing and attaching sequences.

Commands

Address message—Allows you to return to the Address Menu to create more addresses.

attach copy of dos **F**ile—Allows you to attach DOS files to the message being prepared.

attach new i**T**ems—Allows you to attach snapshot items and text, graphics, and DOS files to the message.

display **M**essage—Allows you to display the items in a message that is being prepared. Pops up the Action Menu at this point, so that the items can be rearranged, edited, or deleted.

edit s**U**bject—Allows you to edit the **Subject:** field.

Send message—Sends the message.

Return to main menu—Allows you to jump directly to the Main Menu and ends the actions being performed. If the message has not been stored, it will be lost. You will be prompted for verification.

USING CC: MAIL

Integrating cc:Mail With Facsimile

cc:Mail users can send and receive fax messages if they have the cc:Fax and FaxView optional programs. With cc:Fax, cc:Mail text, graphics, and fax items can be sent. Other items, such as a DOS or Macintosh file, will be stripped from the transmission. With FaxView, users receive incoming faxes directly into their Inbox and display them on their screen—as long as their monitor can display graphics.

Faxes are received by the cc:Mail gateway, which contains a fax card connected to a telephone line designated to receive faxes. When the fax is received, it is encapsulated in an envelope and placed initially in the cc:Mail fax administrator's mailbox. The fax administrator is defined by the cc:Mail administrator and, basically, is an alias for a regular cc:Mail user.

Receiving Faxes

Each page received is stored as a separate cc:Mail fax item, which is designated **x** in cc:Mail. (For reference, text items are **t**, graphics items are **g**, and file items are **f**.) The cc:Mail administrator looks at the first page of the fax, which is typically the fax header page, and then forwards the fax to the intended recipient. The recipient will see the fax as a forwarded message, as shown in Figure E-1.

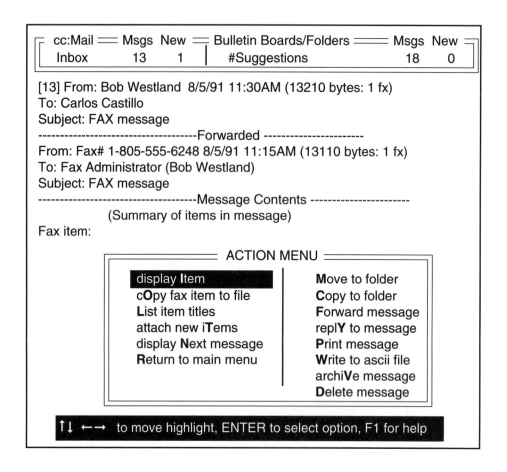

Figure E-1. A fax appearing as a forwarded message

Note: The From: field in Figure E-1 has fax # 1-805-555-6248 as the sender. cc:Mail's fax card knows the recipient's fax machine number, but does not know the actual sender. The **Subject:** field is automatically set to read fax messages.

Viewing Faxes

Fax messages forwarded from the fax administrator can be printed out or viewed on your screen, provided that you have a graphics monitor. The faster the computer, the faster you can view the image. In general, if you do not have a PC/AT or faster, you'll probaby want to print the fax, because the fax image will be displayed very slowly. Mac Plus and SE users will most likely want to print the fax, while Mac II and SE/30 users will probably choose to view the fax on-screen. If the fax is wider than 8.5 inches, it will be truncated (few fax machines can send documents wider than 8.5 inches).

When you are viewing a fax, you can zoom in on an item by pressing the + key or zoom out by pressing the - key. After viewing the item on the screen, press **ENTER**.

Storing and Printing Fax Items

Fax items are treated the same as any cc:Mail item, which means they can be stored and printed using cc:Mail commands. To store a fax item, select the "cOpy fax item to file" command, which will be available only if you have the cc:Fax program. Type in the directory where you want to store the message. If you are using a Macintosh, press the **Store** button and select a file. The fax will be stored in a .PCX graphics format, which means that it can be sent out later as a cc:Mail graphics item or imported into any program that can handle .PCX files.

To print the fax, use the **Print** command. Be patient. A fax typically takes 45 seconds to several minutes per page to print, depending upon the type of printer and type of fax. A graphics file sent to an HP LaserJet connected by a serial cable can take several minutes, while a page of text sent to a laser printer with a parallel port can print in 45 seconds.

Creating Faxes

Faxes are created by using the cc:Mail graphics and text tools, or by any PC program that can save a file in monochrome .PCX format. Files not in monochrome .PCX format cannot be attached directly and sent as fax items: cc:Mail has no way of converting these items to a fax output format, so it strips such files from the fax. If you have a formatted file you want sent as a fax by cc:Mail, you must first print it out on paper and then send it to yourself using a regular fax machine. Once it is received as a fax by cc:Mail, you can then attach it to any cc:Mail message and send it as a fax.

To send a message as a fax, you must first address the item. Fax addresses can be entered in either of two ways. Your cc:Mail administrator may have entered fax machines as regular users. These will be designated as an **r** in the **Location:** field, with the fax number or another reference noted in the **Comments:** field. To send a fax to this machine, just select it as you would any user.

Your cc:Mail administrator will also create a generic fax address, called FAX, which will have **P** in the **Location:** field and the word FAXLINK in the **Comments:** field. When you select this number, a window pops up asking you to enter the specific recipient's name and fax number in the **To:** field of the message as follows:

```
From: Carlos Castillo  8/5/91 12:05AM
To:
Subject:
-----------------------------------------Message Contents ----------------------
None

Address to person at FAX

To: Paul Waldman FAX# 1-818-567-5687




```

Type the name (e.g. Smith, George) and press ENTER, F1 for help

Figure E-2. Addressing a fax

Enter the recipient's name followed by the word FAX# and the actual number, such as:

To: Paul Waldman FAX# 1-818-567-5687.

If your cc:Mail administrator has set up cc:Fax properly, a cover page will be created identifying Paul Waldman as the recipient and you as the sender. The fax will be sent to the telephone number following FAX #.

After addressing your fax, you can use the text editor or graphics editor to create the fax. You can also attach any previously stored text (**t**), graphics (**g**), or fax item (**x**). When you are finished, the fax will be handled as if it were a regular cc:Mail message sent to a remote gateway. The gateway, however, will be a fax machine.

Attaching Fax Items

Suppose a fax item has either been received as a fax or has been saved in DOS as a monochrome .PCX file. If you have cc:Fax and are on an IBM PC or compatible, you will have the "attach fa**X** item" command on your **Attach** Menu. Select "attach fa**X** item" and select the .PCX file, and it will be attached as a fax item.

If you are a Macintosh user, there is no .PCX equivalent designated in the file name. Thus, you cannot attach **.PCX** files to a Macintosh file. To use the Macintosh to attach a fax file, it must first be received by cc:Mail as a fax file.

Sending Repetitive Faxes from any PC or Macintosh Program

There are two reasons you may want to use cc:Mail to send faxes. First, it is convenient when sending a short message to a few people, which means that you would most likely use the cc:Mail text editor. Second, it is a time-saving way to send any fax to multiple recipients—whether or not you can create the fax in cc:Mail.

Let's say you want to use cc:Mail to send a fax to 50 people. Without cc:Mail, you would have to program 50 names in your fax machine, which would tie it up for a long time. You can have cc:Mail perform this for you in background regardless of whether you can create the file directly.

First, create the item to be faxed and print it out as if you were going to send it on your regular fax machine. Second, send it to cc:Mail as a fax addressed to you, so that the fax administrator sends it to your mailbox. Third, readdress the item to as many fax machines as you like, up to cc:Mail's address limit of 200 names per message. You can even create a mailing list in cc:Mail and address the fax item to the list. cc:Mail's fax card will work diligently in background sending the fax as instructed—and will keep a list of who has received it.

Pros and Cons of cc:Fax

cc:Fax is a powerful program that has a number of intriguing uses. While it has its limitations (for example, when receiving faxes, the printer works much more slowly than a regular fax machine and you may find the graphics displayed very slowly on slow PCs) it is a very convenient and powerful tool for sending short faxes or repetitive faxes to a long list of people.

If you are a cc:Mail user, take a close look at cc:Fax, particularly if your fax machine is continually busy and you are already thinking of adding a second fax machine to your office environment. Keep in mind, however, that adding a second fax machine will cost about $500 to $750, while cc:Fax will set you back about $2,000. The additional price must be weighed against the program's ability to send faxes to a list of up to 200 users and to distribute incoming faxes to everyone on the LAN in seconds.

Index

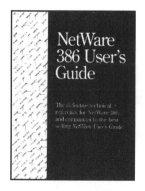

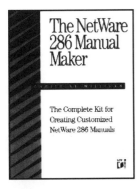
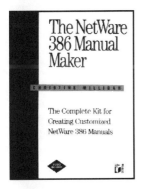

A Library of Technical References
from M&T Books

A Library of Technical References
from M&T Books

Programming in 3 Dimensions
3-D Graphics, Ray Tracing, and Animation
by Sandra Bloomberg

Programming in 3 Dimensions is a comprehensive, hands-on guide to computer graphics. It contains a detailed look at 3-D graphics plus discussions of popular ray tracing methods and computer animation. Readers will find techniques for creating 3-D graphics and breath-taking ray-traced images as, well as explanations of how animation works and ways computers help produce it more effectively. Packed with examples and C source code, this book is a must for all computer graphics enthusiasts! All source code is available on disk in MS/PC-DOS format. Includes 16 pages of full-color graphics.
500 pp. approx.

Book/Disk (MS-DOS)	**Item #218-7**	**$39.95**
Book only	**Item #220-9**	**$29.95**

Fractal Programming and Ray Tracing with C++
by Roger T. Stevens

Finally, a book for C and C++ programmers who want to create complex and intriguing graphic designs. By the author of three best-selling graphics books, this new title thoroughly explains ray tracing, discussing how rays are traced, how objects are used to create ray-traced images, and how to create ray tracing programs. A complete ray tracing program, along with all of the source code, is included. Contains 16 pages of full-color graphics. 444 pp.

Book/Disk (MS-DOS)	**Item 118-0**	**$39.95**
Book only	**Item 134-2**	**$29.95**

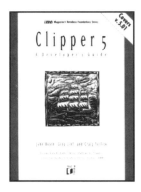

ORDER FORM

To Order:

Return this form with your payment to M&T books, 501 Galveston Drive, Redwood City, CA 94063 or **call toll-free 1-800-533-4372 (in California, call 1-800-356-2002).**

ITEM #	DESCRIPTION	DISK	PRICE

Subtotal	
CA residents add sales tax ____%	
Add $3.75 per item for shipping and handling	
TOTAL	

NOTE: **FREE SHIPPING** ON ORDERS OF THREE OR MORE BOOKS.

CARD NO. _____

Charge my:

☐ **Visa**

☐ **MasterCard**

☐ **AmExpress**

☐ **Check enclosed, payable to M&T Books.**

SIGNATURE _____ EXP. DATE _____

NAME _____

ADDRESS _____

CITY _____

STATE _____ ZIP _____

M&T GUARANTEE: If your are not satisfied with your order for any reason, return it to us within 25 days of receipt for a full refund. Note: Refunds on disks apply only when returned with book within guarantee period. Disks damaged in transit or defective will be promptly replaced, but cannot be exchanged for a disk from a different title.

8054

1-800-533-4372 (in CA 1-800-356-2002)